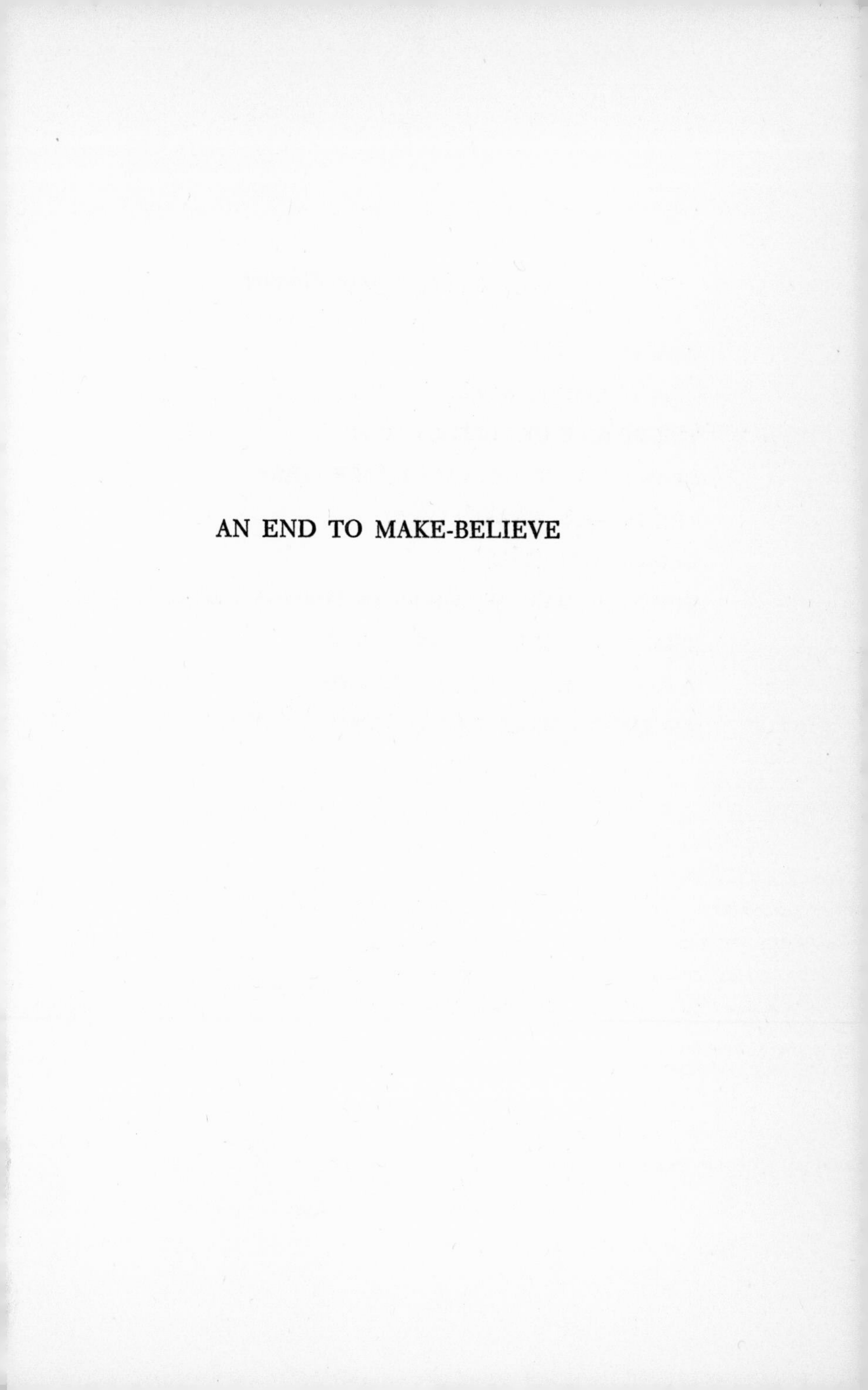

AN END TO MAKE-BELIEVE

Books by Edgar Ansel Mowrer

IMMORTAL ITALY (1922)

THIS AMERICAN WORLD (1928)

THE FUTURE OF POLITICS (1930)

GERMANY PUTS THE CLOCK BACK (1932)

THE DRAGON AWAKES (1938)

GLOBAL WAR (1942)

THE NIGHTMARE OF AMERICAN FOREIGN POLICY (1948)

CHALLENGE AND DECISION (1950)

A GOOD TIME TO BE ALIVE (1959)

AN END TO MAKE-BELIEVE (1961)

An End to Make-Believe

by EDGAR ANSEL MOWRER

"I do not expect that mankind will, before the millennium, be what they ought to be; and therefore, in my opinion, every political theory which does not regard them as being as they are, will prove abortive."

JOHN JAY, first Chief Justice of the United States

Duell, Sloan and Pearce
New York

First edition

Library of Congress Catalogue Card Number: 61-14128

MANUFACTURED IN THE UNITED STATES OF AMERICA

VAN REES PRESS • NEW YORK

To my grandchildren
Diana and Michael Béliard
that they may learn the
price of freedom.

CONTENTS

AUTHOR'S NOTE

Now, as always, the future is with the brave and the purposeful. Good intentions are not enough. Unbeautiful nonsense has prevailed far too long. Further make-believe can lead only to what it sought to prevent—catastrophic war or shameful surrender.

In the sinister game of international poker forced on us by Moscow and Peiping, America has lost hand after hand simply because of half-heartedness. Yet the West still holds the aces. We can win without catastrophe, almost painlessly in fact, once we set our minds and hearts to waging the most important struggle of all time.

Rather than being a history of Soviet-American relations or of United States foreign policy, this book is an analysis of that struggle. It sets forth what this country did and did not do, suggests what it might have done and what I think it should have done.

It contrasts the fanatical ambition of international communism with the unshakeable complacency of most Americans, an opposition of ever more powerful rockets and more intensive propaganda to our concern for the "good things of life"—more money, less work and no worries.

The book concludes with an appeal to all who reject communist slavery to win the Cold War as a prerequisite to establishing a truly free world order.

EDGAR ANSEL MOWRER

Washington, D.C.

ACKNOWLEDGMENTS

I wish to express my gratitude to those who helped me with material, services, suggestions, and/or criticism, and particularly to former United States Ambassador Hugh Cumming; Ambassador George K. C. Yeh of National China; David Sarnoff, Chairman of the Board, R.C.A.; Professor Bernadotte E. Schmitt; Dr. Paul M. A. Linebarger; Colonel Edwin F. Black, U.S.A.; Captain John H. Morse, U.S.N. (ret.); R. B. Forster of the Stanford Research Institute; my colleague Roscoe Drummond; and my wife Lilian T. Mowrer—as well as to various specialists whose positions do not permit them to be publicized. Needless to say, none of these bear any responsibility for the views expressed.

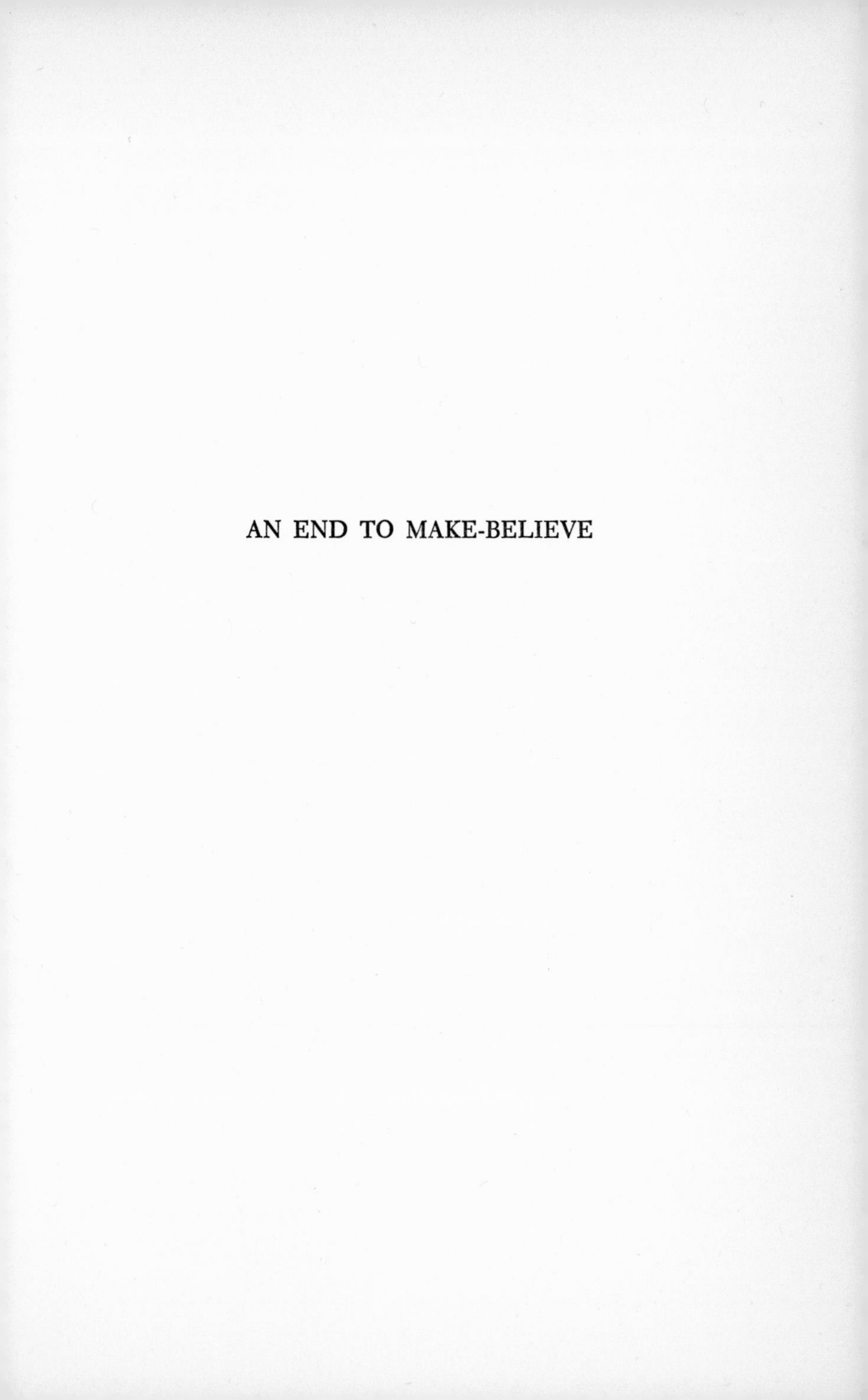

AN END TO MAKE-BELIEVE

Chapter I

COLD WAR

"The trouble with democracy is that it has to wait for an enlightened public opinion."

—Wolfgang von Goethe

Once again, it was the best of times and the worst of times.

The present bulged with achievement and trembled with fear. The future crackled with promise and muttered of doom. Science beckoned new generations into outer space, and frightened them back to the caves.

For a third of the human race the Sixties were a decade of promise, a sunrise of hope, a new start toward a shining but ill-defined goal. But a third of mankind lay under stifling tyranny. Another third, emerging from the long slumber of primitive or simple village life, teetered between the two camps.

In short, it was a time of crisis. History, it is true, is a series of crises, but this one was different. In the past, mankind lived in fear of God's wrath. Now it lived in fear of itself. Its future no longer depended, or seemed to depend, upon forces, divine or diabolic, beyond its control. Now mankind knew its future would be decided by courage, wisdom and compassion.

No one could escape the problems ahead, although millions

tried, by shutting his eyes and walking away. If catastrophe came of crisis, all would be engulfed.

And yet it was a wonderful age as well, great in its achievements, greater still in its potentialities.

Science and its servant, technology, had made the earth a single neighborhood. No part of the planet remained unexplored. The highest mountains had been climbed, the most remote deserts penetrated. Man was boring into the crust of the earth beneath the seas and planning to invade the moon and outer space in the wake of the talking satellites he tossed aloft.

New inventions lightened the burden of physical living. They brought shorter hours and less drudgery. They gave hundreds of millions the highest standard of living that man had ever enjoyed. They also raised expectations and the conception of a "normally" comfortable life. In the West, the gap between rich and poor was slowly but steadily closing. European workmen were shifting from bicycles to motorcycles to little cars. In the United States, an "average" family might own a big car, a small car *and* a motorboat. There seemed no limit to what the age could offer future generations in wealth and leisure.

Medicine had half-mastered man's ancient enemy, physical pain, all but eliminated some of his worst diseases and greatly lengthened his life span. New techniques had enormously increased the amount of available food. True, much of the increase was being absorbed by an explosively expanding population, to the detriment of all. But the promise of plenty was there.

More revolutionary still, thousands, perhaps millions, of persons in the more prosperous countries professed to be disturbed by the growing gulf between rich nations and poor nations, and were doing something about it. The United States was giving economic aid to dozens of countries. The French were leading the world in the share of their per capita income which they devoted to the development of former colonies, with Britain close behind.

To be sure, this charity was not unmixed with self-interest and hypocrisy. The West feared that any failure to care for and develop backward areas would cause the inhabitants to turn elsewhere. Yet whatever their motives, affluent nations were giving on a scale that would have seemed incomprehensibly large to their imperialistically-minded or indifferent parents.[1]

Over large portions of the earth, human bondage in all forms was disappearing. With his insistence upon the right of every people to self-determination, President Woodrow Wilson had sparked a fire that, fanned to white heat for their own reasons by Lenin and his successors, had spread from America to almost every part of Asia and Africa. Soon the age of colonies would pass and each land would be its own master. Color bars between human beings were dropping, and nowhere faster than in the United States.

Despite censorship and repression, a uniform physical civilization was being developed. Cultural differences still remained great, but the trend was toward a single type of industrialized economy.

Moreover, recoiling from the horror of two world wars and the prospects of another one even worse, sovereign states were co-operating as never before. They had created first the League of Nations and then, during World War Two, the United Nations as instruments of social welfare and the peaceful adjustment of disputes. Governments and private organizations were exchang-

[1] "We wonder whether the Cold War may not emerge as one of the greatest boons that mankind has ever known. Certainly, it seems to have been the one force powerful enough to marshal the intellectual and material forces of the United States on a national scale on behalf of the underprivileged and to cause other countries to follow the American lead with programs of their own." Peggy and Pierre Streit: *The Benefits of Cold War,* The New York Times Magazine, Jan. 3, 1961.

ing information in a large number of fields. Cultural and personal exchanges were impressive. Never before had there been so wide and sincere a demand for peace among nations.

All in all it was a time of excitement, of change and of unequaled opportunity for the creative and the adventurous. And to no people did it promise more than to Americans, now finally called upon to extend to all mankind those human and spiritual achievements that were their proud heritage.

Never had there been so good a time to be alive.

Yet conceivably it was just a dream that was turning into a nightmare. For those Western peoples, who alone had the capacity to make the splendid visions real, shrank from the effort. And on the horizon had risen a rival more formidable than the vanquished Hitler. Now Communism stood before the gates, a new scourge of God.

This the Western peoples were all too unready to face. Europe had exhausted itself in two "civil wars" within one lifetime. After 1945, the once conquering European peoples could be led, but for a time, at least, they could no longer lead. Only Americans, spared the worst mental and physical ravages of World War Two, could do that. Yet the United States lacked both the experience and the inclination for a world leadership. Compared with the men of 1783, the leaders from 1941 to 1961 seemed provincials. *They lacked the sense of power politics.*

Moreover, affluence achieved too quickly had softened the American people. At home, they loved politics as a game but they had kept as aloof from the world as they dared. Above all, they sought material improvement for themselves and their children. They did not want to direct or lead foreign peoples. They wanted to be praised, imitated and loved by them.

It was a time when children married and lived on dad; when labor clamored for, and got, an ever larger share of everything the country produced; when capitalists and managers lost their zest for the rigors of competition. Americans young and old had had enough of war, hot or cold, of discipline, danger, power and glory. They wanted to be left alone. A pity that in international Communism they had a mortal adversary.

Looking back over the previous twenty years, an observer could not but note that, however radically the nation had finally departed from its isolationism of the Nineteen Thirties, its leadership had been, in the main, half-hearted. World War Two had been prosecuted with energy, if not enthusiasm. But in Korea the United States had fought only to block and parry, not to win.

Meanwhile, Communism had expanded over parts of first one, then two and finally four continents. Who, an observer wondered, could still deny that the Soviet Union and Red China were not what they appeared to be, that Communism was the repudiation of all that Western civilization stood for, and that its aim was the suppression of freedom, Christianity and *him*?

Bondage and barbarism had advanced to within ninety miles of the shores of America, and still had not been halted. How had this been possible? Why had no one done something?

Chapter II

CORDON SANITAIRE

"All wars are bad but lost ones worst, for then
Comes revolution, making beasts of men."

—PAUL SCOTT MOWRER

According to its intellectual father, Karl Marx, a Communist Russia was impossible. Communism was to displace capitalism only, or first, in the most highly industrialized countries. Marx with his friend and financial supporter, Friedrich Engels, would have been as startled as Woodrow Wilson, David Lloyd George and Georges Clemenceau when, early in November, 1917, word came that revolutionaries led by one Lenin (suspected of being a German agent) were masters of Russia's beautiful capital, Petrograd, and were rapidly taking all power from the democratic provisional government of Alexander Kerensky. How could it have happened?

There had been warnings. For over a century, Russian history had been studded with revolts. Since the Napoleonic wars, "education for revolution" had become a profession of the Russian intelligentsia. Nowhere were such violent rebels. Nihilist terror had become commonplace. If czarist autocracy, established by Ivan the Terrible, had remained intact, this, according to some

Russian historians, was due to the submissiveness of the people after two centuries of quasi-totalitarian Mongol rule. Further, revolutionaries of the twentieth century were badly split—democrats seeking constitutional reforms, Social Revolutionaries brandishing bombs, "Minimalist" Social Democrats urging orderly transition and "Maximalists" under their exiled leader, Lenin, demanding immediate and total change.

Nonetheless, few Westerners were prepared for the events of 1917. That year opened inauspiciously for the embattled Triple Entente. The bloody war of attrition continued unchanged along virtually unchanged lines in France and Italy. In East Europe the Russian steam-roller had smashed itself on German steel. By the middle of the year Russian losses were estimated at *ten million* lives. As usual the Russian soldiers had fought well. But until 1917 they had remained ill-equipped, poorly supplied and miserably led, under the direction of a court honeycombed with pro-Germanism and German agents. The new supplies from Britain and France arrived too late to change their mood. Czar Nicholas II thought no better of democrats than they of him. And despite urging, he refused to relax the autocracy, still less consider abdication even when his soldiers began to desert in droves.

Then in March, 1917, the log-jam broke. After a series of army mutinies, the Czar did abdicate. A provisional government arrested the imperial family. Russia had had a real revolution.

This event looked different in different world capitals. To Berlin it offered a marvelous possibility of victory, to London and Paris the serious danger of putting Russia out of the war. To most Americans, including President Wilson, it was a triumph of freedom over tyranny. What is more, it eased the American President's task of bringing the United States into the war on the side of the Entente.

At least part of the anti-war feeling in the United States grew from suspicion of an alliance that included autocratic Russia. Its move toward democracy enabled Wilson to use Germany's renewal of unrestricted submarine war as the occasion for entering the European struggle and directing it toward enlightened goals. Congress' declaration of war on April 6 delighted London and Paris but did not dismay Berlin. Precisely ten days later, the German General Staff, at the suggestion of the Foreign Office, hoping to promote turmoil in Russia, shipped Lenin back to Petrograd. With his coming, the totalitarian wing of the Social Democrats became the instrument of one of the most daring and effective plotters ever known, far more than a match for the Social Revolutionary fanatics or the moderate Socialists. Lenin was basically an idealist. But, following Marx, he was intent on winning the "historically inevitable" class struggle and establishing a classless society, after which the "state would wither away."

Lenin's contribution was the creation of the most efficient instrument of tyranny ever devised by man: rule by a hierarchical monolithic party under "iron discipline." Its members were imbued with the doctrine of party rule at home and international conspiracy abroad, combining the practices of the bureaucracy of the Peruvian Incas with the tactics of the Sicilian Mafia. Communists believed that they were *justified in doing whatever hastened the inevitable triumph of Communism. There was no other moral aim.* Thereby, Lenin launched one of the most startling political experiments ever known.

What happened thereafter needs no retelling. Within five years the Russian Reds liquidated two provisional governments; concluded a separate peace with Berlin that kept the Germans out of most of their territory; overcame a dozen White military campaigns that were aided sporadically by the forces of *fourteen* other countries; recovered the temporarily lost provinces, with the exception of Poland, the Baltic States, Finland and Bessarabia; survived the worst famine in Russia's terrifying history; concluded a new working partnership with the German Republic; obtained the diplomatic recognition of all principal nations except the United States; and inaugurated the dictatorship of the Russian Communist Party disguised as that of the "proletariat."

Historians and politicians still differ as to why this happened. Some insist on the political immaturity of the Russians, their sheep-like willingness to be led and to believe what they are told by Authority. Others contrast the demonic will of Lenin with the wobbling ineffectiveness of the democrats. Prince Lvov, head of the first provisional government, believed in Tolstoyan non-violence! (Edmund A. Walsh, S.J., wrote that "whoever stops half-way in revolution digs his own grave," a view which much history supports.) Still others believe that the decision of the provisional governments to continue the war dispirited the soldiers and made them and their families easy marks for Lenin's Bolshevik propaganda of peace, bread and land.

Some have thought that if the victorious Allies, during the Paris Peace Conference, had accepted the offer of Chicherin, the Soviet Foreign Commissar, to "name a place and a time for opening peace negotiations with our representatives" and had compelled the reluctant White leaders to go to Prinkipo, Communist Russia might have evolved into a peaceful "evolutionary" member of the international community. (The American chargé d'affaires at Archangel was so disturbed by the bare suggestion of negotiating with Bolsheviks that he offered to resign. At that time the White leaders seemed on the point of winning.)

Or if stronger Western interventionist forces, including Americans, had actually taken part seriously in the White military actions against the Reds everywhere, instead of supplying them and making a half-hearted offensive from Archangel, they might, despite the military skill of Leon Trotsky, have established order in Russia. As it was, foreign intervention only rallied the masses behind the all-promising Reds.

But two things are certain. One is that the Bolsheviks thereafter benefited by the leadership of three exceptional men, Lenin, Stalin and Khrushchev, who backed their unwavering power drive with unmatched courage, a previously unknown mastery of propaganda and a unique singleness of purpose. The other is that democratic governments and their citizens were sharply divided in their attitude toward the young U.S.S.R.

France (particularly Generals Weygand, who later saved Poland from communism, Pétain and Foch) along with Japan, was prepared to intervene and overthrow Lenin. But it was handicapped by its left-wing socialists, some of whom joined the newly organized French Communist Party. Britain under Lloyd George, who at that time favored effective intervention, made an agreement with France to exploit Russian economic resources and employed the unbelievably brave and fanatical agent Sydney Reilly, who insisted that the Soviet Union must be "crushed immediately" if it was not to "overwhelm the human race." Reilly planned the unsuccessful attempt to assassinate the Communist leaders and was eventually killed by them. Lloyd George secretly connived with President Wilson in sending William C. Bullitt and Lincoln Steffens to Moscow with a seven-point peace program and when they returned with Lenin's acceptance, repudiated them. Still later, reverting to his country's traditional suspicion of France, the British Prime Minister repeatedly sought a political and economic accommodation with the Soviets, notably at the Genoa Conference of 1922, where his efforts were thwarted by France's fiery Louis Barthou.

In Germany, socialists and conservatives who had narrowly prevented Communists from taking over, later entered into an agreement with the U.S.S.R. and continued to *finassieren* (Foreign Minister Stresemann's word for his seesaw policy).

Westerners outside their governments were equally inconsistent. How make sense out of two so different revolutions in rapid succession, followed by terror, civil war, outside intervention,

White attempts at counter-revolution, the secession and reconquest by the Reds of several provinces and the wobbles of their own governments?

In Britain, for instance, Winston Churchill was unalterably anti-Communist. On the other hand, the Labor Party tried to prevent the shipment of British arms to help Poland in its war with the Bolsheviks.

Americans, farther from the scene and less sensitive to foreign affairs, judged the emerging Red Bear much as the blind men described the elephant, each according to his sketchy information and personal slant. Woodrow Wilson, though he prevented the United States from formally taking sides, withheld from Lenin the diplomatic recognition he had so quickly extended to Prince Lvov and Kerensky. Most Americans approved his caution. Wilson's State Department remained rigidly hostile. Congress, in October, 1918, passed the Deportation Act and under its terms Attorney General A. Mitchell Palmer waged a campaign at home against alien anarchists and members of organizations advocating overthrow of the government by force or violence. Among his many deportees was the Soviets' first "ambassador," a certain C. A. K. Martens. In fact, the Red Scare of 1919-20 anticipated Senator McCarthy's campaign thirty years later. Many citizens agreed with Palmer wholeheartedly and he could hardly have proceeded without Wilson's approval.

On the other hand, liberals mostly applauded the "aims" of the Communists, while generally condemning their excesses. Yet, they argued, "You can't make an omelet without breaking eggs," indifferent to the number of eggs apparently required and to the taste of this particular omelet. The anarchist, Emma Goldman, looked over the new Russia and found it "hell." But Lincoln Steffens returned to tell Bernard Baruch that he had "been over to the future and it worked," an unconsciously sinister and accurate remark. A former intelligence agent now a business-man, Raymond Robins, who had witnessed the birth of Bolshevism and had applauded, consistently believed that his greatest hour had been when he first saw "the light of hope for freedom from age-long tyrannies and oppression in the eyes of workers and peasants of Russia as they responded to the appeals of Lenin."

Another American later admitted that he too had at this time hoped that the new regime would "eventually become a peace-loving government with a free ballot," which would not interfere with the integrity of its neighbors. He had been Assistant Secretary of the Navy under Wilson and the losing democratic candidate for the Vice Presidency in 1920. His name was Franklin Delano Roosevelt.

Discussion of revolutionary Russia turned on two main points: would the Bolshevik regime eventually evolve into "normalcy"? If not, was it or would it become able to extend its conspiracy to other countries, and eventually to the entire world—its confessed aim?

Soviet leaders proved expert at concealing an exact answer. Yet since they permitted foreigners to enter Russia and were unable to prevent some Russians from escaping, they could not obscure the facts of their society. During the next few years, a remarkable group of permanent correspondents, visiting writers, sociologists and professors, precisely described virtually all facets of Soviet life. In consequence, to those who would read, the nature of the U.S.S.R. was as well known in the Twenties as in the Fifties. Nearly all observers agreed on the basic facts: the new society promised utopia and practiced horror—police terror and torture, slave labor, mock trials, systematic mendacity, brainwashing and the destruction of individual integrity. Its rival leaders fought among themselves like wolves.

Furthermore, the Soviet economy at that time was incredibly weak. This was due partly to the awful devastation of the German invasion, the revolution and the civil war, but also to the leaders' readiness to sacrifice efficiency and the satisfaction of human needs to personal power and their country's military strength. In addition, most correspondents reported, Communist bureaucracy and planning made for poor management. Many felt that without changes such a regime could not last.

Yet at the same time, as good reporters, they noted that the Bolsheviks survived one peril after another, that brainwashing worked, and that given time and luck, Communism might spread. Some observers predicted a future "Red trade menace." Notably, it was precisely those Americans who had gone to Russia most eager to "help build socialism" who became its sharpest critics and repeatedly warned their countrymen of the danger of letting Russia prosper.

On the whole, the American people were not much disturbed, particularly after Lenin's expectation of Communist revolution in other countries proved vain and his successor, Stalin, proclaimed the doctrine of "socialism in one country." Most Americans considered that, while Bolshevism was still an enemy of freedom and capitalism, it was not a particularly dangerous enemy.

Meanwhile, whatever American sympathy for Russia existed would presumably have vanished but for two developments. These were an intense and growing popular dissatisfaction with the outcome of World War One and the emergence of Fascism as an equally repugnant, more obviously aggressive rival to Communism.

Encouraged by Woodrow Wilson to "make the world safe for democracy," millions of Americans who had favored intervention were shocked by his acceptance of the Treaty of Versailles. It was not Wilson's fault. America, even victorious, was not omnipotent. Neither Britain, France nor Italy (not to speak of Japan) had fought the Central Empires in order to reform the world. That, had they been so disposed, they might have sought before 1914. Their primary war aim was to make themselves secure against future German (and, later, against Soviet Russian) aggression by improving their relative positions in Europe and Africa. Since Wilson's League of Nations promised to stabilize this new, more favorable status quo, they accepted it, however reluctantly.

On the other hand, though their half-hearted military efforts to overthrow Bolshevism had failed, all the countries of Europe, with the exception of beaten Germany, spontaneously created around the U.S.S.R. a *cordon sanitaire* to prevent Russian territorial expansion and the spread of the Communist virus. In both aims they were successful. Until 1939 Communist Russia remained on the political defensive and, aside from China (for other reasons), in no place succeeded in creating a Communist party of dangerous proportions.

Wilson counted on his League to overcome the "imperialist blemishes" in the peace settlement which his allies had insisted upon. Not so the Republican Congress in Washington. Elected in 1918, this largely isolationist body found in Wilson's treaty justification for its members' previous opposition to entering the war. Since membership in any international political organization was "intervention," Congress punished Wilson by defeating (1919) ratification of the treaty of which the League "was the heart."

Moreover, the people confirmed Congress' judgment a year later by electing an isolationist President who went to the length of stating, "We seek no part in directing the destinies of the world." His Administration boycotted the League, precisely as the U.S.S.R. was doing.

Thereafter, the United States not only maintained a *cordon sanitaire* against the Soviet Union but also established a second boycott against the League of Nations. The subsequent reluctance of the Allies to pay their war and post-war debts to the United States (except in so far as they received reparations from Germany) further exasperated America's self-righteous xenophobia. For the next two decades a huge country that had outgrown any possibility of isolation avoided its responsibilities by turning its back upon them and denying their existence. President Harding repudiated his former allies and made a separate peace settlement with Germany.

The predictable result was not peace but an era of troubles ending in a new and worse conflict. Isolationist Americans had forgotten, if indeed they ever knew, that much of their past immunity from European political ailments had been due to British naval power. The British fleet had, except when Napoleon III put Maximilian on the Mexican throne, unfailingly protected the Western Hemisphere and maintained whatever world order existed. British sailors and merchants had for a century prospered by serving world peace. After 1920 Britain could no longer fill this role.

Actually the settlement of 1919 erred not in its severity but in its unreality. It was neither conciliatory enough to be accepted by a warlike people nourished on the legend of its own invincibility, nor severe enough to keep that people indefinitely crippled. Either might have worked, but not a compromise that infuriated the German nationalists yet failed to prevent them from planning a new holocaust. Double-dealing German leaders, who managed to elicit the sympathy of many Westerners, shrewdly utilized the West's virtual boycott of the U.S.S.R. to establish secret links with that government. This permitted Germany to circumvent important treaty provisions and laid the foundation for Hitler's rearmament of the nation.

This, however, was something that Western defenders of defeated Germany could not, or at least did not, foresee. Among the worst offenders was the British economist, J. M. Keynes. Whatever future students may ultimately think of his economic theories (the basis of modern consumerism), his book, *The Economic Consequences of the Peace,* became the catechism of the pro-Germans.

Basically, it set forth in a new form a traditional British policy directed at keeping France, or any other European country, from dominating the continent. In this it succeeded admirably. A large section of American opinion, influenced by Keynes, cooperated in removing the few shackles placed upon Germany at Versailles and in rebuilding that country as rapidly as possible into a potential political powerhouse. By the time they caught on, it was too late to do anything but fight. On the other hand, to many liberals, pro-Germanism, popular until 1933, thereafter became identified with pro-Fascism. This confronted the democracies with a dilemma they never satisfactorily resolved.

Fascism was essentially a mass-age nationalism streamlined for aggression. Its founder, the astute former socialist, Benito Mussolini, borrowed the ideas of one-party rule and incessant propaganda from Lenin's Russia, added syndicalist and futurist exaltation of violence, filled the whole with bombastic glorification of the nation-god, in his case, *italianità,* and proclaimed it to be the only complete enemy of Communism.

Since Benito's march on Rome (actually in a train which I happened to share) put an end to three years of intolerable political disorder, the movement won the support of millions of Italians and of jittery reactionaries in the democratic countries. Watching Mussolini's blackshirts efficiently suppress Italy's Communists, labor unions and free-spoken democrats, they hardly noticed that the new movement was far closer to Bolshevism than to any sort of genuine democracy.

On the other hand, many democrats recoiled with such horror from the injustices, brutalities and crude warmongering of the Fascists that they began to feel a hitherto unnoticed sympathy for Lenin's and Stalin's "economic democracy." Just as President Wilson was unwilling to choose between Soviet Communism and White reaction in Russia, Westerners found themselves embarrassed by the problem of dealing with two enemies. How decide between them? Perhaps the isolationists were right after all and the wise course for America was to ignore Europe and "Europe's eternal wars."

For twelve years successive American Administrations stood firmly by the policy of no diplomatic recognition of the godless Bolsheviks, faithfully supported by the East European Division of the State Department. At first this boycott applied to trade as well. In 1921 Secretary of State Hughes stated that short of "convincing evidence" that Moscow had restored private property, the sanctity of contracts and rights of free labor, the United States saw no basis for considering trade relations. A year later Secretary of Commerce Hoover, who had learned a lot about the Soviet regime while helping fight the Russian famine, insisted that trade with Russia was more a "political than an economic" question.

As a compromise the United States permitted the U.S.S.R. to set up an agency called Amtorg, through which many American firms sold machinery, metals, cotton and motorcars while importing manganese, furs, flax and caviar. Through Amtorg Moscow also recruited American firms and specialists for the reconstruction and development of Soviet resources and industry.

Otherwise, Soviet political overtures were steadily rebuffed. Fearful of the capitalist intervention Lenin had foretold, the Soviet Union was the first state to ratify the Kellogg-Briand Pact outlawing war. Yet when, in 1929, Secretary of State Henry L. Stimson charged Russia with violating that pact in fighting against the Chinese in Manchuria, Foreign Minister Litvinov asked defiantly just how the United States "deemed it possible to give advice and counsel to a government with which it maintained no official relations."

The change came with the Great Depression.

Chapter III

BETWEEN TWO ENEMIES

"The friendship of the peoples of Germany and of the Soviet Union, sealed by blood, has every reason to be lasting and firm."

—Joseph Stalin to
Joachim von Ribbentrop
December, 1939

Less than five weeks before Franklin Delano Roosevelt took office as President of the United States, a nationalist fanatic called Adolf Hitler had become Chancellor of Germany. Within a month Hitler had destroyed parliamentary democracy, burning the Reichstag as a symbol of the fact, and made Fascism, called in its German version National Socialism, the most explosive factor in the contemporary world. For his basic purpose was nothing less than to overthrow the Soviet Union, unseat Britain as Europe's leader and make the Third Reich the most powerful country on the planet.

Few Americans, outside of a handful of newsmen in Germany, recognized this fact or what it might portend. Certainly not the new American President, although he hated aggression. For he had other far more pressing problems. The chief of these was the

Depression, which had transformed the American social climate more than anything since the Civil War.

The American people had, by and large, accepted previous depressions as part of the scheme of things, simply to be endured. But the Depression of 1929 was far more severe in depth and duration. Managed prices, labor unions and one-crop agriculture prevented rapid self-cure. Industrialization had deprived most individuals of any chance of riding it out on their own.

Yet there was something else. For with the exception of the Germans, industrialized peoples elsewhere withstood almost equal misfortune with far less mental anguish.

Clearly, Americans had changed. Progress—ever upward, bigger and bigger, more and more—had become America's God-given right. Instead, forced sales, wholesale bankruptcy, joblessness for millions and tightened belts for all but the few who had foreseen the storm and reefed their sails in time.

Actually, almost nobody went hungry. The living standard in the United States at the bottom of the Depression was approximately that of "prosperous" Britain in 1960. The difference was, of course, that whereas Britons rose to this level, Americans had fallen to it. Many developed a sort of psychosis that led them to despair of the foundations upon which their country had been built.

Private initiative had failed, they felt, and something else was needed. Here was the origin of the subsequent welfare state. But to many inflation sufferers, Roosevelt's skill in keeping a modified capitalism afloat by discarding considerable laissez-faire ballast was not enough. They wanted a complete break with the rotten present—technocracy or democratic socialism (the "middle way") or (why not?) the great Russian experiment. Among those demanding change, the most emotional were certain Evangelical preachers, an odd lot of reformers, radical labor leaders, underpaid and inadequately respected professors, other intellectuals and the young, who could see no future for themselves.

Here was the "capitalist breakdown" Communists had been expecting. They took full advantage of it. Creeping from obscurity, a smug "we told you so" on their lips, they worked their way into circles and positions where previously they would not have been tolerated. They rose to the top in labor unions and in some cases were able to keep "traitors to the Party" from getting jobs. They operated all sorts of liberal organizations and "popular fronts." They sneaked into government positions where they could not only influence decisions but could keep their second home, Moscow, informed of all that went on.

Above all, they concentrated on young people starting life, many of whom were pushovers for smooth-talking, well-trained Red agents. Where they could not function openly, Communists disguised themselves as liberals. By a perversion of language later to be immortally depicted as Newspeak ("War is peace. Freedom is slavery.") by George Orwell (*1984*), they seized and denatured their opponents' most sacred words. Red tyranny became "democracy," or, at least, "economic democracy." Fanatical Chinese Reds emerged as "agrarian reformers."

The Party also managed to organize cells among "public-opinion molders"—Hollywood writers, actors, musicians, and, above all, in universities, just how many nobody knows. These were the days when Alger Hiss, Julian Wadley, Harry Dexter White and many others were secretly recruited and placed in key listening posts. Disguised Communists even managed to reach a few softhearted business-men, embittered by their own bankruptcy or by the suffering they saw around them. How could one not admit that American society had failed?

Even more effective was the comparison of "peace-loving" Russians with aggressive Japanese militarists and European fascists.

In 1931 the long-restless Japanese led off by seizing Chinese

Manchuria. The naval disarmament treaties negotiated by Republicans in the early Twenties in order to keep Japan quiet proved to have made that country almost immune to military interference in its own waters. Secretary of State Stimson's policy of not recognizing forceful conquest got nowhere. Japan was getting ready to create an Asian "Co-prosperity Sphere" or bust. Nazi Germany and Fascist Italy soon followed suit in taking up aggressive policies.

Many in America began to view the U.S.S.R. as a stabilizing force in both Asia and Europe. Senator Borah had previously argued that there would be no peace in Europe until other nations ceased to treat the U.S.S.R. as an outlaw. It was, Borah insisted, impractical to try to separate a people from a government that was "improving their lives." Now he advocated diplomatic recognition of that government by the U.S. as a brake on aggression. Some depression-ridden American exporters, hoping to revive their diminishing trade with the Soviets ($100 million in 1931, $9 million in 1933), heartily backed the proposal.

There was opposition. Notably, Paul Scheffer, a famous German newsman, who knew Russia better than many Communists, warned that American recognition "could only provoke Communist Russia to greater . . . attacks on bourgeois European countries."

Before his election in 1932 Franklin D. Roosevelt had pretty well made up his mind to grant recognition to Russia if the American people gave him the chance. According to Sumner Welles, he had "thoroughly studied foreign relations" in the previous years. He had decided on his Ambassador to Moscow, namely, William C. Bullitt, Wilson's and Lloyd George's emissary to Lenin during the Versailles Conference in 1919.

Bullitt still believed that, in exchange for recognition, the U.S.S.R. was ready to drop certain policies obnoxious to Americans and go some way toward a just settlement of the Czarist debts. Certainly, once elected, F.D.R. quickly dropped the previous Republican policy of cold-shouldering the "bandit regime" in Moscow and set about convincing the Kremlin of America's desire for friendship. Despite bitter opposition in the Department of State, which had voluminous records of Soviet inhumanity and hostile intentions toward all non-Communists (some of which records F.D.R. later ordered destroyed), Secretary Hull believed that there was a good chance of a satisfactory arrangement.

In November, 1933, Soviet Foreign Minister Maxim Litvinov came to Washington and the United States and the U.S.S.R. signed a six-point agreement which the President assured a sceptical Jim Farley "would work out all right." Bullitt departed the following spring for Moscow with what some have called the "pick of the U.S. Foreign Service" as his staff. Some Europeans applauded, others were baffled by the completeness of the "peaceful revolution" in the United States.

The first honeymoon was short-lived. It took the astute Bullitt less than six months to reverse his favorable view of the Russian regime. That same autumn he returned to Washington and reported verbally to the President that he had been "completely wrong" about the Kremlin's readiness to behave as a normal government. The U.S.S.R. neither paid its debts nor stopped Communist propaganda in the United States. In fact, at the Seventh All-World Congress of the Communist International (1935), American Communists turned up officially.

Yet on this point the President was deaf. Useful as he found Bullitt later, notably as Ambassador to France from 1936 to 1941, the President virtually ignored his warnings about Soviet ambitions. Thereafter, he made his own Russian policy with some encouragement from liberals at home.

Meanwhile growing fear of Nazi Germany and militaristic Japan was driving the Kremlin into a new zig—seeking international respectability. Stalin sought and obtained membership in the League of Nations. There his representative, the ever-flexible Litvinov, preached collective security in and out of season. He volubly advocated "total disarmament," something which other delegations knew would, if carried out in Russia, bring down the Bolshevik regime within a few months. Stalin ordered foreign Communist parties to cease defaming democratic socialists, hitherto their chief targets, and try to form "popular front" governments with them.

In order further to soften up the democracies, whose aid he needed if he was to survive, Stalin in 1936 bestowed upon his grateful subjects their second "constitution," described as "a million times the most democratic in the world." Along with exhortation to obey the laws, it contained a number of promises: the right of each citizen to work, rest and security. It guaranteed him freedom of speech, of the press, of assembly and of street processions and demonstrations. It declared "inviolable" his person and his home. It granted the right of secession to every "Union Republic." It was, in fact, a noble document except for a curious flaw: above the governmental organization it described, stood, *unmentioned*, the all-powerful Communist Party under a dictator who did whatever he pleased.

Comrade Bukharin, believed to have written much of the document, was murdered two years later by Stalin, perhaps as a warning against taking the new constitution too seriously. In any case, it was never applied. Justice in the U.S.S.R. continued to be a travesty. Nonetheless, George Hicks, a British Member of Parliament, called it "an enormous advance on what has ever been embodied in the fundamental laws of any country previously."

In the same year (1936), Stalin offered to France a formal military alliance, doubtless in the hope that it might give pause to Hitler's bellicosity. The French, perhaps unwisely, refused.

Alone among governments, the U.S.S.R. openly provided arms

and "volunteers" for the originally democratic socialist Spanish Republic, whose adversaries, the Franco nationalists, were in open rebellion. True, in the process, Stalin laid his hands on the Republic's gold reserve, made orthodox Communism the leading forces in its armed forces and brought about the murder of the Trotskyite Communists of Catalonia. These were no small gains. Moreover, with Britain, under the cover of "nonintervention," successfully preventing wobbling France from doing much for the Republic, Stalin got the reputation of an active anti-Fascist, endearing himself to millions otherwise unsympathetic to Sovi Communism.

For, meanwhile, systematic aggression by Germany and Japan was casting an ever blacker shadow over the democracies. Why did the latter not bestir themselves? The trouble was that leaders in America and other free nations differed violently over what should be done. For centuries Britain had thrived on a policy of keeping continental Europe divided. After 1919 it supported beaten Germany against France, occasionally followed in this policy by the United States. As a result, in 1933, an undeterred and revived Germany chose Adolf Hitler. Similarly undeterred, British conservatives then evolved a plan for scotching the Soviet danger by allowing Nazi Germany to expand into Eastern Europe regardless of French disapproval. This policy, conceivably harmless if adopted in favor of a Germany governed by the democratic Weimar Republic, became, with Hitler on the prowl, a reckless gamble.

France, thanks to Germany's defeat and the Russian Revolution, had for a few years enjoyed a sort of primacy in Europe. It had earned this by its immense war effort and superb courage. But once victorious, successive French governments sought to maintain that primacy with a minimum of effort and with purely defensive military forces. As a result, except during the premiership of Raymond Poincaré, Britain, with American assistance, half-coerced, half-argued France into a series of surrenders: the decision to let Germany recover economically under the Young Plan; premature allied evacuation of the Rhineland; non-intervention in the Spanish Civil War; finally, the disastrous Munich decision to permit Nazi Germany to annex the fortified rim of Czechoslovakia by "negotiation," provided it refrained from the use of force. What is more, an influential French group headed by Pierre Laval approved this course, and took the lead in preventing effective action against Italy's aggression in Ethiopia.

On the other hand, it was precisely in the years that he was doing most to attract sympathy abroad that Stalin pushed his own terror to its most bestial lengths. Taking as a pretext the assassination of his favorite stooge, Kirov, the Kremlin tyrant purged the Communist Party leadership of all those comrades of Lenin who, he felt, might endanger his personal rule. Some of them were murdered in prison (presumably because they refused to confess imaginary crimes). Others, charged with some sort of conspiracy, appeared at carefully staged trials during which they pleaded guilty of crimes they certainly had not committed.

Before World War One, the Sultan Abdul Hamid of Turkey had horrified the civilized world by the systematic slaughter of his closest associates. Compared to Stalin's butchery of his former friends, that of the insane Turk was mild. Among Stalin's trial victims were many of Russia's best generals. To be sure, some Americans, including Ambassador Joseph E. Davies, took this sinister judicial mummery seriously. But many others, who had not previously realized that Stalin's U.S.S.R. was basically lawless, were shocked by the murderous fraud, the charges of fantastic crimes and the unbelievable "confessions" by one-time leading Communists.

Conflicting international developments further divided the

United States. On the one hand were those who bitterly reproached Britain and France for not standing up to Fascist aggressors, if necessary with Soviet help. On the other were those who shuddered at the moral monster in the Kremlin while refusing to recognize that Nazi Germany, Fascist Italy and Japan were, respectively, in the hands of a paranoic, a self-intoxicated histrion and a group of military megalomaniacs. Not stopping the aggressors could mean ultimate war for America. Stopping them might result in opening the gates to further expansion of Godless Bolshevism.

Thus while some Americans enlisted to fight Franco in Spain, others, notably Roman Catholics, forced the Administration into strict application of neutrality in the Spanish Civil War, even though such an attitude was patently a contribution to the rebels, who were well supplied with arms by Germany and Italy.

Disgusted with both Fascism and Communism, yet terrified of being ultimately involved in their clash, Congress then sought safety by locking the American people in the cellar of neutrality and throwing away the key. Influenced by honest but gullible fanatics who believed that the United States had been duped and bribed into entering World War One by American armament makers ("merchants of death") and by American creditors of Britain and France, Congress, with the President reluctantly assenting, passed the Neutrality Acts, which included an embargo on arms sales. Thus they hoped to prevent both themselves *and their descendants* from ever being siren-sung into another "foreign war."

Thereby they made World War Two virtually certain. For although the Axis leaders were rash, they were not stupid. They knew that the United States had tipped the balance in favor of the Entente in World War One and could do it again. The passage of the Neutrality Acts convinced them, as Secretary Hull had foreseen, that America would not again intervene in Europe, at least not soon enough to thwart their ambitions.[1]

They misjudged the American President. By this time, the White House had become the center of a group who saw less danger in Soviet Communism than in Fascism. The President had always had a certain sympathy for both Russian revolutions and undoubtedly considered that while the Kremlin's means were evil, its aims were good. Eleanor Roosevelt's great heart made her a pushover for fast-talking reformers. Certainly, by 1937, F.D.R. had come to believe that America's vital interests simply forbade allowing Germany to take over Europe or Japan to close China to the West. Cautiously he started doing whatever he could in the face of the Neutrality Acts he himself had signed. Late in 1937 he put up, unsuccessfully, a trial balloon: a suggestion that the United States should join other peace-loving peoples in "quarantining aggressors." This was a development of the Stimson Doctrine of nonrecognition of territories acquired by force.

Shortly before, disregarding Bullitt's repeated unsolicited warnings, F.D.R. had sent Joe Davies as Ambassador to Moscow with instructions to assure Stalin of American friendship.

Roosevelt's cautious effort to get Congress to amend the Neutrality Acts to permit the sale of arms to chosen governments got nowhere. Yet even with their hands so tied, he and Hull did what they could. While protesting against each Axis act of aggression, they subtly urged resistance on Britain and France, a task made no easier in London by the sympathy of the American Ambassador, Joe Kennedy, for Britain's policy of appeasing Hitler. Even while F.D.R. was congratulating the Western powers on keeping the peace at Munich (1938), Hull recognized that the agreement

[1] Nazi Germany's plan of expansion in East Europe was revealed to me in Moscow, in December, 1936, by the local head of German intelligence, a Navy captain. He based his confidence in the plan's success on the "certainty" that the United States would never again participate in a European conflict.

would further convince the Axis powers that they had little to fear from the "decadent" democracies. And both F.D.R. and his Secretary of State wondered why, with Hitler preparing for war, Chamberlain and Daladier had made no serious effort to bring the U.S.S.R. into the Munich negotiations and, if necessary, into a direct military understanding that might keep the Axis quiet.

For the Munich "settlement" speeded up aggression. In March, 1939, Hitler, in a second bite, took the rest of Czechoslovakia. Britain and France faced armed conflict with little hope of outside support. Congress still opposed any revision of the Neutrality Acts. The U.S.S.R., pretexting its cold-shouldering by the West at Munich, withdrew into silence. (Ambassador Davies had predicted that Munich would "drive Russia into an economic and ideologic agreement with Hitler.")

Toward the end of March, 1939, Chamberlain gave a unilateral British guarantee to Poland. A few days before (March 10) Stalin had talked of friendship with Germany, warning the Anglo-French "warmongers" that the U.S.S.R. would not pull their chestnuts out of the fire. He then dismissed Litvinov after nine years as Foreign Minister and replaced him with the anti-Western Molotov. Britain and France reluctantly sought to reopen negotiations for a defensive alliance with the U.S.S.R., but just as at the time of Munich, Stalin's price for any alliance with the West was the right of free access to the countries between the U.S.S.R. and Nazi Germany, namely, Poland, the Baltic States and Rumania. Poles, Balts and Rumanians said no. They were convinced that once inside their boundaries, the "Soviet hordes" would refuse to withdraw without leaving local Communist governments behind. Neither F.D.R. nor Hull "felt any disposition to bring pressure to bear on Poland" (Hull's words).

So while British and French emissaries in Moscow halfheartedly sought some compromise with Molotov, Germany and Russia announced the signature of a ten-year nonaggression pact, and secretly signed a protocol partitioning Poland. The United States, informed of the coming agreement a few days in advance, could do nothing but exhort the European governments to keep the peace.

In vain. As expected by most governments, and certainly by American newsmen in Europe, Hitler invaded Poland (September 1, 1939). Seventeen days later, Soviet forces dashed in like hyenas, and seized those parts of wounded Poland allotted them by the Nazis.

Still another shock to most Americans. Without Stalin's complicity, Hitler might not have dared start the war. Although some, including Joe Davies and Harry Hopkins, considered that Russia, cold-shouldered by Britain and France, had acted in self-defense, this was not the prevailing opinion. Many who had embraced Communism, or played with it, or trusted Russia, turned away in disgust. Stalin was no better than Hitler.

Yet although American opinion swung almost unanimously to the side of Britain, France and Poland, the majority still stubbornly insisted that this was no war of ours. The same individuals who subsequently condemned the U.S.S.R. for attacking Finland and applauded the League of Nations for expelling the Soviets, simultaneously criticized Britain and France for ten months of military immobility.

Roosevelt, according to Hull, was now sure that preventing a German victory was vital. But how? Although Congress had not insisted on his invoking the Neutrality Acts against Finland, the United States was committed to neutrality. Just what F.D.R. thought of Russia is not sure. It seems probable that he agreed with Hopkins and Davies that the Allies had brought Soviet hostility upon themselves.

Hitler's blitz of France in June, 1940, and the appalling readiness of many Frenchmen to collaborate with Hitler through fear of Bolshevism and distrust of Britain were severe jolts to American complacency.[2] Few Americans had realized that between the two World Wars the peace-loving French had created an army so defensive in character that it was unable to take the offensive successfully.

From then on the President, Hull and Secretary of War Stimson moved, with all requisite stealth, from strict neutrality to aiding the Allies by "all means short of war." They sought—vainly—to persuade the Soviet Ambassador in Washington that a Hitler victory would be also a disaster for the U.S.S.R. The White House secretly encouraged the work of the newly formed Committee to Defend America by Aiding the Allies. In March, 1941, the Administration steered the Lend-Lease legislation through Congress, and saw to it that the U.S.S.R. was not excluded as a possible later recipient.

One day in May, 1941, when I was in the State Department as a newsman, Assistant Secretary Berle invited me into his office. He looked at me intensely for a moment: "What would you say if I told you that Hitler intends to attack Soviet Russia in the near future?"

"I would say that Hitler is a bigger fool than I took him for. It cannot be possible."

"You will see," said the Assistant Secretary. And on June 22, 1941, Adolf Hitler ordered his victorious forces to crash through Soviet-occupied Poland and conquer Russia.

That attack changed everything. For Nazi Germany it meant almost sure defeat. To Britain it offered the prospect of salvation. To the U.S.S.R. it meant a life-and-death struggle but, in case of victory, the chance of another great step toward world dominion.

This much was obvious to both Churchill and Stalin, though not to Hitler or Roosevelt. To F.D.R., Germany's invasion of its

[2] In Bordeaux, the day after the French Cabinet had decided on what amounted to surrender, Pierre Laval insisted to a dejected American correspondent that France's "only enemy" was the Soviet Union.

former friend meant the chance of securing Hitler's defeat short of war—as he had promised the American people. There is no evidence that he seriously considered the danger to the world from too complete a Russian victory. Or if he did, he put it aside as secondary. And there is also no evidence that he ever accepted the real situation as it was in June, 1941: *the world was divided not into two but into three, basically irreconcilable camps.* Fascism, to be sure, was the enemy of both Communism and democracy. But the sated, pacifist and divided democracies were the enemies and intended victims of *both* Fascism and Communism. Morally there was little or no difference between the two totalitarian creeds. Both were predatory and expansive, not because of their rulers' personal ambitions, but by their natures. Each knew that ultimately the one or the other must succumb. The question was, which would eat the other. To overcome Stalin, Hitler, though the stronger, needed the neutrality or preliminary defeat of Britain and France to avoid the kind of dreaded two-front war in which the Kaiser's Germany had been beaten. Since Britain and France would not remain neutral he cunningly first sought the Kremlin's benevolent neutrality while conquering France and immobilizing Britain, then turned his victorious forces against his secretly hated confederate in the Kremlin. Had he previously eliminated Britain as he eliminated France, the plan might well have succeeded.

Stalin had no interest in assisting the democracies to defeat Nazi Germany unless thereby he could expand Communism. Otherwise, a successful democratic coalition might later join the East European states in a new *cordon sanitaire*. Instead, he succeeded in provoking what he hoped would be an equally matched war between Nazi Germany on one hand, and Britain and France on the other, in which both sides would bleed themselves white, leaving him master of Europe. Hitler's 1939 offer of a nonaggression pact, plus the secret agreement giving him a first bite of East

Europe, was music. Yet Stalin erred twice: first in overestimating the strength of the two European democracies, and then in demanding too much "compensation" for his neutrality and military supplies, which gave a victorious Germany an excuse for attacking him.

Both Hitler and Stalin erred in supposing that Americans would remain neutral while they, with their Japanese confederate, divided the world. But their partnership between August, 1939, and June, 1941, made it clear that basically World War Two was a *triangular* struggle, each side essentially against the other two, with any alliances merely temporary groupings.

Chapter IV.

THE THREE-CORNERED WAR

"It requires a very unusual mind to undertake the analysis of the obvious."

—ALFRED NORTH WHITEHEAD

Within hours of Hitler's attack on the U.S.S.R., Churchill promised Stalin all possible military aid. To hard-pressed Britain that attack offered a first clear prospect of victory without the kind of mass slaughter that characterized World War One. Although British losses in that war were smaller than those of France (not to mention Germany or Russia), the memory of them was still a nightmare in Britain. In consequence, Churchill, until the inevitable Allied landing in France, 1944, favored the peripheral strategy open to the side that commanded the seas.

But against the powerful German armies, such a strategy could succeed only if at some point some other country engaged the larger part of the German forces. Hitler's selection of Russia as his next victim was therefore a gift from heaven to the British. Thereafter, on the Allied side, the Russians did most of the fighting and dying, and, considering their equipment, did magnificently.

Moreover, Britain's conscience was clear. Russia's plight was the direct consequence of Stalin's own tricky behavior in 1939. But although Churchill owed Stalin no gratitude, he felt immense relief. His business thereafter was, with America's help, to get enough supplies to the Russians to enable them to keep on fighting and to resist the temptation to make any sort of separate peace with Nazi Germany.

Here Churchill found a kindred spirit in the American President. F.D.R. also favored giving massive aid to Russia "with no strings attached." He obviously preferred keeping American and British losses to the strict minimum compatible with victory. Without the Russian mass resistance this would be impossible. In exchange for extensive Lend-Lease benefits to the U.S.S.R., he counted on full Soviet assistance, even in the final conquest of Japan.

On one point Churchill differed sharply from Roosevelt. F.D.R. (as he confided to his son Elliott) went along with his advisers in believing that the defeat of Germany would inevitably leave a vacuum in Europe into which "neither English-speaking power can move permanently." Theoretically the United States could, of course, maintain occupation forces until a reviving, partially federated or closely allied Europe was able to fill the vacuum. That would prevent or restrict Soviet expansion westward, a desire passionately shared by the European peoples without exception.

But this the President did not think American isolationists would accept, at least not for "more than two years." Nor were they, he believed, likely to support an active American policy in Europe after the war. Think how they had abandoned Europe after World War One! And how could he, having, with a massive assist from the Japanese, overcome their resistance to participation in another European war, justify keeping a large American force over there for perhaps decades? So he decided that, come what would, "no American soldier should go east of Trieste," and resisted all of Churchill's efforts to make him change his mind. If such a decision left East Europe open to Soviet expansion, well, some other method of limiting this would have to be found. Anyhow, nobody could maintain that countries like Poland, Rumania and Yugoslavia (which last the President thought should be divided) had known much of democracy.

His eventual choice of method was a Great Design, a world peace plan with Soviet participation, thanks to which the Anglo-Saxon countries could both benefit by maximum Russian resistance to the Nazis during the war and, meanwhile, induce Stalin to relinquish further Communist expansion.

By holding out the benefits of such a plan F.D.R. felt sure he could, in consequence, "handle Stalin" as the imperial-minded Churchill could not. Nor did the President despair of succeeding until, at the earliest, shortly before his death in April, 1945.

The Great Design grew gradually in his mind. At the Argentia, Newfoundland, Conference with Churchill in August, 1941, he spoke to Elliott only of "organizing" peace "for many generations" under the supervision of three or four Great Powers who would control the strategic keys of the world. Within such a scheme France, considered by Roosevelt as no longer a Great Power, would relinquish Bizerte and Dakar and Turkey would share the Dardanelles with Russia. Lesser countries might be disarmed. This conception later broadened into the vision of a new world organization, of which the fighting United Nations would be the nucleus. In previous years Roosevelt had wobbled on American membership in the League of Nations, being first for and then against. But early in World War Two, perhaps under the influence of Secretary Hull who considered a new international organization abolishing spheres of influence as the key to peace, the President also placed his hopes in a new League of Nations. In this body the four, later five, victorious Great Powers could exercise world-wide authority through a council, while lesser countries let off steam within a fairly academic assembly. Such a scheme required the military participation of the U.S.S.R.

But there was more. In addition to defeating the Axis and creating a new world organization, the President undertook to liquidate all colonial empires. At Argentia he informed a scandalized Churchill: "I do not believe that we can fight a war against fascist slavery and at the same time not work to free people all over the world from a backward colonial policy." To his son Elliott he stated: "The colonial system means war," and, at a later date, "Don't think that Americans would be dying in the Pacific tonight if it hadn't been for the shortsighted colonial greed of the French and the British and the Dutch." Therefore he planned to strip France, the Netherlands and, in theory, Britain of their colonies. (Why he overlooked Portugal, Spain and Belgium is not clear.)

Admittedly, he lacked any evidence that the war reflected colonialism except in so far as the Axis powers were patently trying to acquire colonies. And since he never applied the theory to the Soviet empire, he did not need Stalin's actual help here. Still the argument "colonialism equals imperialism equals war" had been a favorite theme of Lenin. American liberals of the Thirties had imbibed freely of socialist doctrine and the President considered himself a liberal. Abolishing colonialism (outside the U.S.S.R.) was sure to appeal to the Kremlin.

In 1941, the President set out to woo Stalin away from world revolution by several methods. First, he would give Stalin all possible military aid without asking any counterpart. No matter how insolent, difficult or demanding the Russians might become, no matter how much his own agents in Russia might complain of shabby treatment by the people they were helping, he would keep on unperturbed until Germany was defeated.

Next he planned to let Stalin see that he was doing what he could to lighten the dark image of the Soviet Union in the eyes of the American people. He gave the requisite instructions to the

Office of War Information. He had the State Department issue a document testifying to the "improved" position of religion in the U.S.S.R. He sent his defeated Republican rival to the 1940 election, Wendell Willkie, around the world, chiefly to urge friendly participation in a future world order on the Russians. Willkie's subsequent book, *One World,* became a major vehicle of the President's Great Design—an indivisible peace with Soviet participation. He even gave what support he could to a film based on the earlier diary, observations, personal letters and carefully censored diplomatic dispatches of his former Ambassador to Moscow, Joseph E. Davies. The portrait of Red Russia presented to millions of Americans was, to say the least, "highly retouched." Nonetheless, the Administration's efforts at prettying up the dark reality of the Soviet Union were so successful that many Americans forgot all they had learned from those early correspondents in Moscow.

The President's third device for reforming Stalin was to refrain from siding with his natural ally, Churchill. Roosevelt personally liked Churchill and respected Britain, but he had an ineradicable suspicion that the Prime Minister was trying to conduct the war in a way that would enhance Britain's position when it was over. He complained to Elliott at the Teheran Conference (1943): "Trouble is, the P.M. [Churchill] is thinking too much [sic!] of the postwar and where England will be. He's scared of letting the Russians get too strong. . . . Maybe the Russians will get strong in Europe. *Whether that's bad depends on a lot of factors.*" (My italics.) And again to Elliott, after that conference: "The biggest thing was making clear to Stalin that the United States and Great Britain were not allied in one common bloc against the Soviet Union . . . making sure that we act as referee, as intermediary between Russia and England." Elliott concurred enthusiastically.

So did Roosevelt's "own personal foreign office," Harry Hopkins. The latter constantly urged his boss to "deal personally with

Stalin" and not give the impression of "leaving Russia out in the cold." In 1942, answering American complaints of Soviet secrecy, Hopkins boasted that "the United States is doing things for Russia which it would not do for other United Nations without full information from them." And at Yalta (1945), even after the Soviet had revealed its innate imperialism in occupied Rumania and Bulgaria, Hopkins slipped a note to the President:

"I think the Russians have given in [sic!] so much at this conference that I don't think we should let them down. Let the British disagree if they want to."

Robert Sherwood records that the American liberals who felt they had won the 1944 election had become "increasingly suspicious of Churchill's apparent determination to restore the unsavory status quo in Europe." In any case Roosevelt ostentatiously went out of his way to convince Stalin that however Churchill felt about the U.S.S.R., he, Roosevelt, was a reliable friend.

Moreover, to bring the Roosevelt charm to bear as soon as possible, the President repeatedly suggested a personal meeting. But the Georgian proved too much for him. He declined all invitations until his victory at Stalingrad had almost totally destroyed his military dependence on the United States. Actually, at his first meeting, in Moscow in 1941, with Hopkins and Harriman, who had come to inquire what military assistance he needed, Stalin had "appeared to be more anxious to discuss future frontiers and spheres of influence than negotiate for military supplies." He did not *ask* for, he *demanded* a second front in Europe immediately—and, not getting it for almost three years, spoke of Western treason. Hopkins seems, however, to have been so successful in convincing him of Roosevelt's support that the Georgian reached the conclusion that he headed the alliance. Certainly, as Ambassador Harriman warned, Stalin expected to do so at the end of the war.

Meanwhile, the President's fifth and final method of seeking his confidence was first to postpone and then gradually to concede the Soviet Union's successive territorial demands.

To be sure, the President realized he might fail despite all his efforts. As he admitted to Forrest Davis in December, 1943, he was gambling upon his ability to convince a fanatical Communist nurtured on a heady mixture of unlimited personal power, Russian nationalism and a quasi-religious belief in the victory of Communism that he should thenceforth abjure the last and cooperate with his "class enemies."

Stalin might "prove unappeasable," but Roosevelt simply saw no good alternative to appeasing him. In consequence, in the words of Robert Sherwood, "the repeated warnings of possible Russian perfidy that Roosevelt received in 1941 and throughout the years that followed, served only to make him increase his efforts to convince the Russians of America's incontestable good faith."

In point of fact, Roosevelt had been warned indirectly by none other than Stalin himself. At the Atlantic Conference in August, 1941, F.D.R. met Churchill alone and, after giving him the usual lecture on British imperialism, signed with him the Atlantic Charter, which became the theoretical basis of the fighting United Nations. The terms of that agreement indicated a double purpose —to mollify American objections to helping Russia (this was before Pearl Harbor) and to act as a check on imperialism.

The key articles of the Atlantic Charter read as follows:

1. The [signatory] countries seek no aggrandizement, territorial or other.

2. They desire to see no territorial changes that do not accord with the freely expressed wishes of the peoples concerned.

3. They respect the right of all peoples to choose the form of government under which they will live; and they wish to

see sovereign rights and self-government restored to those who have been forcibly deprived of them.

Now in 1939, the Soviet Union, as the hyena of Nazi Germany, had seized the Baltic States, part of Poland and part of Rumania. Then it made war on Finland and annexed a chunk of Finnish territory. Obviously such "territorial changes" had not been made according to the "freely expressed wishes of the peoples concerned." Yet in December, 1941, after Pearl Harbor, Stalin informed Britain's Foreign Secretary Anthony Eden that he intended to keep all the territories he had acquired with Hitler's aid, and some of German East Prussia as well, and that Britain's consent to this should be incorporated in any treaty of alliance between the two countries. In other words, the Atlantic Charter's injunction against further aggrandizement must apply *after* June, 1941. Yet fearful of losing Stalin's cooperation, Eden was in favor of accepting those demands.

Communicated to Washington, they caused a scandal. I remember the consternation on the face of Under Secretary of State Sumner Welles, when, early in 1942, he showed me the list of Russian demands. Any official acquiescence in them would, at that time, have turned the American people against Stalin to an extent dangerous to the wartime alliance. Roosevelt therefore put his foot down and after a series of Anglo-American discussions, informed Britain that the United States would not recognize any such agreements as binding. All territorial changes must wait until the end of the war. Yet in the succeeding months and years he accepted all of them and more—piecemeal, gradually, almost invisibly behind a cloud of diplomatic secrecy and ambiguous communiqués. For he felt he had to.

The clearest explanation was given by that bluff executive, Secretary of War Stimson: "The central decision of World War II was that it must be fought as an alliance as close as possible with

Great Britain and Russia. Not once during the war was this decision questioned. The three nations, in American eyes, formed an indispensable team for victory over Germany. Together... they could not lose. Apart, or at cross-purposes, or with one of them defeated, they could hardly win. It was thus the constant purpose of the American Government to do all that would achieve and cherish a cordial unity of action."

Unity of action in defeating Germany was, however, one thing. Bribing Stalin with others' territory to drop the purpose of world revolution and become a pillar of the peaceful postwar world was quite another. Could one accomplish the first without the second? The President's advisers said no.

It is hard to recapture the confidence which led American leaders, despite repeated rebuffs, steadily to "bet that the Soviet Union needs peace and is willing to pay for it by collaborating with the West."

Harry Hopkins, the man F.D.R. relied on most, had even more confidence in Stalin's good intentions than did his boss. Hopkins gave his personal favor to Davies (and tried to persuade him to return to Moscow as Ambassador) and in Moscow chose Colonel (later Brigadier General) Philip R. Faymonville as his representative. Davies and Faymonville had distinguished themselves by their faith in the master of the Kremlin. Hopkins' policy was simple: "Russia must be considered as a real friend and treated accordingly and... personnel must be assigned to Russian contacts that are loyal to this concept."

After Yalta, Hopkins told Sherwood that "the Russians had proved they could be reasonable and far-seeing and that there wasn't any doubt in the minds of the President or any of us that we could... get along with them as far into the future as any of us could imagine."

Hopkins was, of course, the rankest amateur in world affairs. What of the professionals? Secretary of State Cordell Hull backed the President's "hunch" about Stalin from the beginning. Once he got Stalin's consent to enter the planned new United Nations (at Moscow in October, 1943), he felt satisfied and sharply repudiated subsequent suggestions that "we should cut off Lend-Lease supplies to Russia unless she made a settlement with Poland." True, in 1944, he was momentarily disturbed by Ambassador Harriman's report of the Russians' apparent expectancy that "their strength would enable them to dictate conditions." But he noted that "President Roosevelt and I saw alike with regard to Russia . . . we felt we could work with Russia."

The quick-thinking Roosevelt frequently skipped Hull and dealt directly with Under Secretary Sumner Welles. The latter, a logical and experienced professional, was under few illusions about the Soviet Union. Yet he too condemned the earlier *cordon sanitaire* that had stopped Communism for almost two decades. For Russia was, Welles noted, "potentially the strongest power in the world" and could become either the "greatest menace the world has yet seen" (prophetic) or "the greatest force for peace and orderly organization in the world." Since it had "at least temporarily abandoned world revolution as a means of establishing the supremacy of Communism," the United States should be willing to give it frontiers with a view to its "essential security."

Secretary Hull's successor, Edward R. Stettinius, echoed Hull. James F. Byrnes, who became Secretary of State after Stalin's perfidy had become evident to some in the Administration, considered that the Yalta meeting had demonstrated that the Big Three could "cooperate in peace as in war."

These were Democrats. Important Republicans felt much the same. Roosevelt's beaten rival for the presidency, Wendell Willkie, returned from his visit to Moscow, with full trust in Stalin.

The man who had most to do with the U.S.S.R. in the military field, Stimson, found the Russians "in their way, magnificent allies." Stimson "admired the colossal achievement of the Soviet armies and the skill and energy of the Soviet leaders," was "not disposed to contest the Russian claim that there must be no anti-Russian states along Soviet borders," and "saw no reason for the United States to be upset by the fact of Russian strength."

As late as March 31, 1945, after the Soviet had broken its agreement in at least three Balkan countries, General George C. Marshall informed the Supreme Commander in Europe, General Eisenhower, that "the single objective should be quick and complete victory," apparently regardless of political consequences. Eisenhower thought that "overshadowing all goals for us Americans was the contribution we might make locally toward establishing a working partnership between the United States and Russia." The future American President saw no reason why two systems should not exist peacefully side by side.

A high-level military estimate submitted to the Quebec Conference (August, 1943) stated that Russia's postwar position in Europe would be dominant. With Germany crushed, "there is no power in Europe to oppose her tremendous military. . . . It is essential to develop and maintain the most friendly relations with Russia."

Admiral William D. Leahy was no exception. The Admiral, who accompanied the President to all the important conferences and was privy to all that went on, had no illusions about the U.S.S.R. Yet he thought that "involvement in European politics would inevitably bring us into another European war" and "had no qualms" about the "so-called concessions to the Russians." After all, Russia was doing the most fighting; had made no separate peace with Germany; had come to an agreement with France, Poland and Yugoslavia; and had promised to enter the war against Japan, which the Admiral did not think was necessary but which pleased the generals. What else did we want? Why quibble about payment? With so much official support for his major policy, Roosevelt must have felt he could hardly be wrong.

Public opinion, too, was mostly on his side. In a significant little volume, *U.S. Foreign Policy 1943,* Walter Lippmann reasoned that at the end of World War Two the Soviet Union would be either the ally or the antagonist of the United States and Great Britain. There was no possibility of re-establishing the East European cordon against Russia. Germany had broken it and the U.S.S.R. could do the same. Since the United States "could not promise to defend the East European states," he wrote, they must be neutralized. Our concern was not with European but with world affairs. Britain and Russia had the same fundamental interests. The United States and Russia had never quarreled. Therefore, the United States, Lippmann argued, should seek a *nuclear alliance* with Russia as well as Britain. How better express the President's purpose?

Against such a current, the wartime doubters could do little. Some high State Department officials led by Assistant Secretary Adolf A. Berle, along with ex-Ambassador Bullitt, protested. Like the American ex-correspondents, Eugene Lyons, Demaree Bess, William Henry Chamberlin and Isaac Don Levine, they based their view of Stalin's intentions on personal experience.

No less than three consecutive wartime Ambassadors to Moscow, Lawrence Steinhardt, Admiral William H. Standley and Averell Harriman, uttered repeated warnings. The last wrote (April 4, 1945), "Unless we and the British adopt an independent line, the people under the areas of our responsibility will suffer and the chances of Soviet domination will be enhanced." The highly respected former Ambassador to Japan, Joseph C. Grew, who became Under Secretary of State in December, 1944, officially stated (May, 1945) that "as a war to end wars, this war will have been futile, for the result will be merely the transfer of totalitarian dictatorship and power from Germany and Japan to Soviet Russia, which will constitute in the future as grave a danger as did the Axis." In fact, Grew predicted that the Soviet would take Mongolia, Manchuria and Korea "into its orbit" to be followed in due course by China and eventually by Japan. All in vain.

Not even Winston Churchill could prevail against the stubborn President. How hard did he try?

Far harder than he made public at the time. The Prime Minister had no illusions about the nature and ultimate purposes of the "sullen, sinister Bolshevik state" he had once tried to strangle at birth as the mortal foe of civilized freedom. Yet he was handicapped by Britain's and his own basic positions: his country needed the Soviet Union's massive military effort far more than the United States; and he was opposed to ordering the kind of costly operations that had characterized the battles of World War One. A breach with Russia simply had to be avoided. So in 1942 he signed a twenty-year alliance with Stalin.

At first, as the head of the weakest of the three allies, Churchill tried to be hopeful. Like Roosevelt he looked forward to three-power control of the world. He favored giving German Köenigsberg to Russia as a warm-water port, since "government of the world must be entrusted to satisfied nations." At one time (1943) he believed that Russia "would concentrate on reconstruction for the next ten years. . . . Communism had already been modified. I thought we should live in good relations with Russia." For if left outside a world organization Russia would become the "power center of another group." Within it he thought the unanimity rule would "make it impossible for Russia to embark on courses not approved by the U.S.A. and the U.K."

Thereafter, judged by his own book, *The Second World War,* he was continually drawn in the opposite direction. He recognized that Russia's danger was for the time Britain's danger and that, however unintentionally, the two were allies. Yet unlike Roosevelt, he did not believe that the European "power vacuum" following Nazi Germany's defeat need be filled by Russia and he struggled manfully to revive "the glory of Europe, the parent continent of the modern nations and of civilization." He wanted to fill the vacuum with a European confederation without Russia.

Each time the President acquiesced in a particular Soviet grab, Churchill yielded, but as little and as slowly as possible. He conceded to the hungry Bear those Baltic States it had already eaten; then he accepted the Soviet's right to East Poland; next, the Soviet frontier of 1941 rather than the prewar line of 1939. And in the face of F.D.R.'s startling insistence that no American soldier should go "east of Trieste," Churchill unilaterally tried to save half of the Balkans by making a deal with Stalin. Yet it was Churchill who had first insisted on dumping nationalist Mikhailovitch for Communist Tito in Yugoslavia.

Churchill eagerly adopted Roosevelt's original suggestion of a secondary invasion of Europe through Trieste and the Ljubljana Gap to Vienna, only to be blocked by the President, who dropped the idea lest it provoke Stalin. When the Prime Minister found he could not prevent the amputation of East Poland, he suggested "moving that country westward" at the expense of Germany. For he realized that in East Europe Stalin could, without some binding agreement, take almost anything he pleased.

Above all, despite Churchill's admiration for the Russians as fighters, he judged that the U.S.S.R. had brought invasion upon itself by aiding Hitler in 1939, that it had been willing to "share the booty with Hitler," and that Russia and its Western Allies *were not fighting the same war.*

Churchill urged first Roosevelt and then Truman to keep up "steady pressure on the Russians." He urged Eisenhower to "shake hands with the Russians as far east as possible." In fact, the Prime Minister never forgot that Russia was a "mortal danger" that could be diminished only by reaching "a settlement with the Russians before the armies of democracy melted."

In 1945 Churchill tried hard to bridge the "deadly hiatus between the fading of F.D.R. and President Truman's grip of the vast world problem." He saw the situation clearly. Harry S. Truman was one of the bravest and most patriotic of American Presidents. But few have ever come to the White House with less preparation for such a world crisis as he was supposed to resolve. Lacking personal experience in world affairs, Truman inevitably relied upon the close associates and advisers of his predecessor. They had no use for Churchill's attempt to "politicize" the war operations or for his by now complete distrust of Stalin's intentions.

So when Churchill advocated American occupation of Prague and Berlin, Truman turned down both suggestions on the advice of his military advisers. Eisenhower thought Berlin of little importance and General Bradley was afraid of the casualties its capture might involve. Yet Churchill persisted, and in a message to Truman (May 12, 1945) spoke of "Soviet misrepresentations" and how "an Iron Curtain is drawn down upon their front." Would not the American President insist on its being raised? He would not. Truman insisted only that the United States "must not let itself be dragged into antagonism with Soviet Russia." He also turned down Churchill's next plea that, since the Russians were breaking all pledges in the Balkans and in Poland, the Americans should not retire west from the Elbe to the permanent occupation line until satisfied about these places.

For the rest of 1945 Truman stood by F.D.R.'s basic policy: to obtain Russia's future cooperation in world peace the United States must refrain from any sort of too close partnership with Britain, the country from which it had derived its language, basic political outlook and a large part of its literature and law.

The result was foreseeable, though not to most Americans.

In his more than twelve years in the White House, Franklin Delano Roosevelt had changed the United States more than all of his predecessors since the Civil War. He had recognized the imperialist threat of the Axis and met it as early as the American people would permit. He had made the United States the strongest power on earth, with a monopoly of the atom bomb. He had organized a new world organization through which he hoped to secure world peace. Yet this consummation was prevented by much the same mistake that Woodrow Wilson made at Versailles —the sacrifice of concrete power to the hope that an international organization would replace the previous power struggle.

Why did Roosevelt fail? Was the emergence of a triumphant and domineering Russia the inevitable consequence of beating Germany and Japan, as many Americans still insist? Or could it have been avoided by greater wisdom and imagination?

Churchill's answer (March, 1945) was that the United States "stood on a scene of victory, master of world fortunes but without a true and coherent design."

Yet a Great Design was just what Roosevelt had. Furthermore, he pursued it coherently. To discover where he went wrong it is necessary to examine the validity of his basic assumptions.

The first of these, which Churchill shared, was that the United States and Britain needed the full military assistance of the Soviet Union to defeat, first Nazi Germany and then Japan, *without suffering unbearable military losses.* Against this, at least until the end of 1944, when the Anglo-American armies crossed the Rhine, there seems to be no valid argument. Whether without the successful manufacture of the A-bomb, which came too late to count in the decision, the English-speaking leaders needed Soviet help to finish off Japan is much disputed. Certainly they purchased that assistance dearly.

F.D.R.'s second assumption was that to obtain maximum Russian aid, the West must prevent Stalin from making a separate peace with, or ceasing to fight against, Hitler by giving him virtually everything he wanted. This was correct only when Stalin became free to do either. Hitler's main political aim was the conquest and colonization of the Soviet Ukraine. Short of such an acquisition it was almost inconceivable that the Fuehrer would have consented to any separate peace or truce with a half-beaten Stalin.

Stalin's regime could not, moreover, have withstood the political shock of yielding the Ukraine to Germany. Before he could have considered a separate peace or even a truce with Hitler, the Georgian had to reconquer all his 1939 territories. This he accomplished only by June, 1944. *Until that date, the West could count on his full assistance not upon his terms but strictly upon its own.*

During three years Roosevelt and Churchill could with relative impunity have "ganged up" on Hitler's former confederate and tried to induce him to renounce publicly any claim either to any extension of his power or social pattern beyond his 1939 frontiers. This they could if necessary have "encouraged" by reducing shipments of essential supplies (over ten billion dollars' worth from America alone) until he conformed. Had he later reneged on his promises and started on his career of European conquest, they might well have taken the risk, once their own troops had crossed the Rhine, of dispensing with his further military cooperation. The Germans, seeing a split, would have preferred peace with, even occupation by, the West. Moreover, when it became evident that even without German connivance, the Anglo-Americans could have beaten the Russians into Berlin and most of Czechoslovakia, they might have confronted Stalin with the choice of seeing them remain there or of re-establishing non-Communist regimes in Poland and the East. Either would have been preferable to what they got.

Such action was, however, incompatible with F.D.R.'s third assumption. This was that the Soviets would inevitably move into the power vacuum created by the German collapse. Churchill properly dissented. The kind of East European confederation planned by him would have, with British and American backing, probably been able to withstand Soviet pressure.

But such backing would have conflicted with the President's decision to send no Americans "east of Trieste." That attitude automatically made East Europe a Soviet sphere of influence unless the President could buy off Stalin by a more attractive offer. There is no evidence that the President felt any deep compunction (as Churchill did) about turning over anti-Communist Poles and others to the tender mercies of the Red dictator. Ambassador Averell Harriman characterized such Soviet control as the "barbarian invasion of Europe." Apparently his chief lost no sleep over such a prospect. After all, diplomatic reports of 1943 and 1944 gave reason to hope that in the future, as in the past, Russians and Americans could pursue their respective policies without clashing.

A further Presidential assumption was that the U.S.S.R. was a state like others, with limited political and ideological objectives. F.D.R. was unconcerned by its publicly proclaimed aim of world rule—an ambition that surpassed Hitler's. Nor for all the President's insistence on liberating his European Allies' colonies does it seem to have dawned upon him that, of all existing empires, the U.S.S.R. was the largest, with the most, and worst treated, colonies. How he could sternly reprove Churchill for imperialism without speaking even more harshly on the same topic to Stalin is hard to understand. But neither he nor his closest advisers, outside the neglected State Department, possessed more than an amateur's knowledge of international affairs.

A basic misunderstanding of the nature both of Soviet Communism and Communist philosophy led Roosevelt to the final fatal assumption upon which he gambled his wartime policy, namely, that he could "handle Stalin." He sincerely expected to transform a fanatical Communist and power-mad despot into a public-spirited leader of a peaceful world community. On this assumption he placed his great stake—and lost. Yet in justice to a great President one must admit that Roosevelt's wishful thinking was that of most of his nation. For while Americans were familiar with ruthless business leaders, they rarely met political extremists, if only because American politics are not ideological. The United States had never been ruled by either a fanatic or a true *Machtmensch*.

Defenders of Roosevelt still argue that allowing Russia "friendly neighbors" was the right policy if only Stalin had "kept his promises." Yet of Stalin could be said only what the judge said of Huckleberry Finn's pap, that he "reckoned a body could reform the old man with a shotgun, maybe, but he didn't know any other way."

Since the U.S.S.R. and its two Western Allies were not fighting the same war, the latters' best course was not to get along with Russia but to try to compel Russia to get along with them, and restrict its gains to the barest minimum.

Chapter V

STOPPING THE RED TIDE—AT ONE END

"Truman was the first one who ever said 'no' to anything Stalin asked."

—*The Forrestal Diaries*

President Truman inherited an approaching military victory over the Axis and an almost completed international organization, the United Nations, which would be able to keep the peace as long as the U.S.A. and the U.S.S.R. were in agreement. He further inherited a monopoly of a new weapon, the atom bomb, a number of which would make the possessing country potentially supreme on earth.

Politically he might still have retrieved a good deal that Roosevelt had gambled away. Rapid and drastic action might have righted a badly compromised situation in East Europe and the Far East. But once he ignored Churchill's three desperate appeals —to occupy Berlin and Prague before the Russians; to stay on the Elbe until Stalin restored satisfactory regimes in Poland, Rumania, Bulgaria and Hungary; and after that, to keep a large garrison in Central Europe—he could do little in the West.

In the Far East, only a complete reversal of F.D.R.'s policy of making the Chinese Nationalists cooperate with the Communists could have prevented a victory by the latter.

Failing to act promptly and drastically in both areas, Truman was left with nothing but his own courage and the A-bomb threat to use in stopping the spreading Red blight.

In consequence, as one of the critics of F.D.R., former Ambassador William C. Bullitt, described the victorious United States of 1945: "We stood like the most powerful creature that ever lived, the carnivorous Tyrannosaurus Rex, who had a body the size of a locomotive, teeth a foot long and a brain the size of a banana."

For it soon developed that the same political conflict that had made the new international organization necessary had rendered it almost as impotent as its predecessor, the League of Nations. Despite the encomiums that greeted its birth, the United Nations remained a glorified vigilance committee, unable to enforce against powerful malefactors what little international law existed.

On the other hand, the four-year monopoly of the A-bomb soon gave the United States military supremacy such as no nation had ever possessed. Once he was in possession of several such bombs, Truman could have summoned the Soviet Union to withdraw all its armed forces within its 1939 frontiers—or else. A contemporary argument—that in the event of the total destruction of Russia's cities and productive machinery by A-bombs, vast Soviet armies might have holed up in undestroyed Europe and occupied Manchuria and raided neighboring countries or destroyed the countries they occupied—seems pure fantasy. How could they have lived in destroyed areas? Such armies would speedily have found themselves short of war matériel, food and everything else they needed. How could they have resisted the temptation to go home and try to save what was salvageable?

Nor could it be rationally argued that use of A-bombs against Communist enemies would have been morally worse than against Japanese aggressors. The Soviet's cannibalizing of Poland and Yugoslavia, for example, with Czechoslovakia to come, was no whit less reprehensible than Nazi Germany's or Japan's assault on civilization.

The difference lay not in the potential act but in the minds of the American and allied peoples, beginning with the American President. Harry S. Truman came to high office convinced "peace in the world would not be achieved by fighting more wars." And anyhow, as he cogently argued (*Memoirs,* p. 91) in 1945 and 1946, all thoughts of a war to make Russia retire "would have been rejected by the American people before they were even expressed."

The American people were relaxing in a double victory and urging their President to "bring the boys home" forthwith. Like their wartime leaders they considered every "foreign war" as a murderous but necessary football game which of course had to be won. Thereafter, their instinct was to kick over the adversary's goalpost and go home to Thanksgiving dinner. Despite all their big talk about the "American Century" and being the "most powerful nation in the world" (two expressions which had been better forgotten), they were, as Navy Secretary Forrestal ruefully observed, not only uninterested in new power but eager to divest themselves of the wartime strength, now reinforced by the A-bomb, which they had created by such effort and expense.

Moreover, regardless of the Soviet's persistent outrages, the common victory had created sympathy for Communist Russia in all Western countries, including the United States.[1] Only the East

[1] Speaking before the National Council of American-Soviet Friendship (!), November 14, 1945, Assistant Secretary of State Dean Acheson said: "To have friendly governments along her borders is essential both for the security of the Soviet Union and the peace of the world."

European peoples, who had also dreamed of peace and freedom and found themselves the victims of a new and equally hideous tyranny, were bitter beyond words.

As F.D.R.'s wartime Assistant Secretary of State, Adolf Berle, Jr., put it: "Millions of men and women were uprooted or delivered into the hands of their enemies, were condemned to concentration camps or perpetual exile. Vast numbers of these were not defeated enemies, in whose case revenge might be emotionally understandable. Many had struggled at terrible cost to overthrow the Nazi regime. Their reward was horror worse compounded."

National China, shaken to its foundations, needed wholesale American backing to survive.

Yet the fact was, Westerners everywhere were quite ready to forget everything they had previously known about the nature of Soviet Russia and support their hard-fighting but incurably imperialistic ally's insistence on having "friendly neighbors." To this seemingly reasonable demand, Communists, fellow travelers, ultra-liberals, reforming clergymen and doctrinaire intellectuals added the never-ending charges that such faithful allies as Chiang Kai-shek and the Polish colonels (who had suffered the first onslaught of the Axis without surrendering) were financially corrupt or Fascist at heart and deserving of little sympathy. Some American State Department officials in China reported that Chinese Communists were likely to "provide a better government" than the Nationalists, who had "lost the confidence of the Chinese people." (What a Red China would do not only to its own people but to the United States was beyond their ability to foresee.)

Few Americans protested when General Eisenhower handed back to Stalin, to be imprisoned or executed, some 135,000 Russians whose crime consisted in having preferred the (unknown) monster in the Wilhelmstrasse to the criminal in the Kremlin. The American people, from the President and Eisenhower down, were paying dearly for their twenty-year return to isolationism

(1920-1940), when they might have been learning about the world they were now compelled to lead.

In fact, as Under Secretary of State Joe Grew complained, not only most Americans but "elements in government" remained "woefully blind as to the fundamental philosophy and doctrine of the Soviets. . . . Our people as a whole were blind to the Soviet doctrine that the end always justifies the means, that the Soviets feel warranted in entering any commitment, making any promises, concluding any treaty or agreement without the slightest intention of honoring such commitments when they run counter to what Moscow considers the best interests of the Soviet Union. They were blind to the ruthlessness of the Kremlin toward the individual and to the savage cruelty with which any defection from the communist 'line' is punished. They were blind to the Soviet doctrine that communism and capitalism cannot continue to exist peaceably side by side, and that war between the two camps is eventually inevitable. They were blind to the patent fact that the only language understood by the Kremlin is the language of strength, force and power; that friendly appeasement in any form is regarded as a clear sign of weakness and an invitation to further demands or encroachments."

Truman, like Roosevelt, was an ardent New Dealer, eager to give all peoples more of the "good things of life." He probably had less faith in the Russian Communists than Roosevelt. But he shared F.D.R.'s liberalism and deep-rooted anti-colonialism, believing with him that every people, regardless of its cultural and political development, had a right to cast off foreign rule and manage its own affairs. Why should he not? After all, few Americans realized that they, descendants of white settlers, were nothing if not successful colonialists who had killed off or exiled the original "savages" and shamelessly taken the Southwest from its Spanish and Indian (Mexican) owners. In fact, as one embittered Englishman noted, the United States, in encouraging natives to rebel against their white masters, was not, as it imagined, taking sides with General Washington against the British Redcoats but supporting Sitting Bull against Custer. Yet since few Indians and Mexicans remained in the United States to protest, while in other places the white colonists remained a small minority, it was easy for Americans to overlook their own past imperialism and condemn their democratic allies. Certainly Truman did. During his first years in the Presidency he used his influence to get the French out of the Levant, the Dutch out of Indonesia and the British out of India, Ceylon and Burma as rapidly as possible.

As late as 1945 some Americans still felt that the real danger to future peace remained *British* colonialism. Just as F.D.R., in March, 1945, was still grousing about Britain's readiness to "let the United States fight Russia," so thereafter Senator Claude Pepper soberly warned his country against "guaranteeing British imperialism." Nor was Truman any more keen-sighted than his predecessor in discerning Soviet Russia's extensive and cruel colonialism behind the smoke screen of Soviet anti-colonial propaganda.

Truman certainly did nothing to discourage his countrymen's anti-colonialism. For his *Memoirs,* written after he left office in 1953, record his belief that what principally has "cast a shadow over our lives" was inaccurately termed the "Cold War." Really it was "a period of nationalistic, social and economic tensions. These tensions were in part brought about by shattered nations trying to recover from the war and by peoples in many places awakening to their right of freedom. More than half the world's population was subject for centuries to foreign domination and economic slavery."

This was a half-truth. Imperialist Communism was obviously one form of social and economic tension and social change. But that is not what Truman meant. He felt that even without Communist pressures and Soviet armed support and manipulation, the colonial peoples' legitimate demands for independence and the good things of life would have caused the contemporary political crisis.

This is I think inaccurate. For without Communist incitement and support, undeveloped peoples, however rebellious, would simply have lacked the military power to free themselves or the political leverage to elicit economic aid from outside. They would have had to rely on nuisance value, such as the Indians used in convincing their British masters to set them free. Britain would have evacuated its Egyptian bases only when it felt ready to go; an armed seizure of the Suez Canal by Egyptians would have been impossible. Indeed, without the Cold War—the irreducible conflict between two powerful camps—there would have been no Far Eastern crisis, no dangerous Arab problem, no great African upheaval. Instead, there would have been a slower and far healthier liberation. The virulence of the colonial crisis, whether in Laos, Cuba or the Congo, was a direct consequence of an ideologically and militarily divided world.

The overwhelming cause of world tensions was simply Communist determination to impose economic and political tyranny upon unwilling peoples.

Inevitably, Truman's first nine months of office were among the busiest and most trying that ever an inexperienced statesman faced. For a few months he hardly realized his problem. Back from his first international conference at Potsdam (July-August, 1945) he confided to me: "They told me I would have trouble with Stalin. I had no trouble with Stalin. I got everything I wanted from Stalin."

Undisturbed, he set about consolidating the peace. Despite a certain personal reluctance and Secretary Forrestal's protest, he yielded to the popular clamor for rapid demobilization. After all, as he described it later, "Americans are . . . spontaneous and . . . headlong in their eagerness to return to civilian life." Instead of preparing to use his monopoly of super weapons to right a badly compromised situation, he proposed, under proper safeguards, turning them over to the United Nations and so getting rid of them. His main concern was convincing the Soviet Union that it had nothing to fear from the United States. At the end of some months, despite his growing awareness of the Soviets' intentions, he reduced the defense appropriation for 1946-47 from about forty to eleven and a half billion dollars. And as late as the end of 1946 he was eager to lend Stalin—on proper terms, of course—a billion dollars for reconstruction.

Most important of all, the President, confident in the United Nations' ability to preserve peace, and still unaware that America's vital interests were being steadily undermined, liquidated the wartime alliance at a time it should have been perpetuated and broadened to balance the expanded Soviet empire. In Britain, Churchill was out and his successor, Clement Attlee, feared that any attempt to create a solid front in Western Europe would be considered as a hostile act by Stalin.

While the United Nations Relief and Rehabilitation Administration was distributing (mostly) American assistance to Communist governments that used it to tighten their hold on their unhappy peoples, Truman cancelled Lend-Lease to his allies. This was explicable in the case of the U.S.S.R., which had never been a real ally. But it aggravated an economic crisis in war-exhausted Britain (which, to Truman's credit, he almost immediately alleviated by an immense American loan). Also, he flatly refused to share with Britain the secret of manufacturing the A-bomb. Considering that this weapon was largely the offspring of a marriage of European science (German, British, Danish, Italian, French) and American money and technique, and that British scientists in particular were party to everything but the mechanics, such a refusal compelled bitterly impoverished Britons to duplicate American procedures at great cost of time and money.

Yet Congress saw no reason not to sever that wartime "foreign entanglement" which many legislators had only reluctantly accepted in the first place. The President was in no mood to elude Congressional control had he been able to do so, which is uncertain. In consequence, the wartime coalition simply disbanded. To be sure, in March, 1946, Truman "approved" Winston Churchill's speech at Fulton, Missouri, in which the former Prime Minister appealed for continuing the "fraternal association" of the English-speaking peoples; correctly accused the Soviet Union of desiring the fruits of war without fighting; and suggested forcible intervention against further Soviet imperialism at a later time. But neither Churchill nor Truman followed it up and such "association" with Britain as continued was less than fraternal.

For nine long months the President and his Secretary of State, James M. Byrnes, strove by every means in their power to preserve a working partnership with the U.S.S.R. In vain. By this time the post-war situation was approximately as follows:

The Soviet Union had swallowed the three little Baltic states; annexed a large section of pre-war Poland and the northeast corner of pre-war Germany, Rumanian Bessarabia and two slices of Finland. It had, in addition, pushed Poles into a broad segment of East Germany, from which there could be little hope of ever removing them, short of more violence. Russia was well on the way to setting up Communist regimes in Poland, Hungary, Rumania, Bulgaria, Yugoslavia and Albania. It had, by arrangement with the West, occupied the eastern forty per cent of the remaining Germany and had installed another slightly camouflaged Communist government. It was nourishing a Communist revolt in Greece and preparing similar revolts in France and Italy. It was threatening to seize the Dardanelles from Turkey. It was seeking a voice in the control of the West German Ruhr and a mandate over Libya. In addition, it was stubbornly refusing to evacuate northern Iran.

In the Far East, Soviet troops (at the invitation of F.D.R.) had occupied Chinese Manchuria, re-establishing, with Washington's acquiescence, outposts in Port Arthur and Dairen. The Chinese Reds had been armed for their take-over of that giant country. Russia had occupied the Japanese portion of Sakhalin Island and the strategically important Kuriles. The Kremlin had angled for a voice in the control of Japan (which Truman wisely made purely nominal). It had seized and installed a Communist regime in the northern half of Korea.

Rarely has any war given one of the victors such vast spoils to use against its former allies. In short, the Soviet Union, previously a vast but impoverished and outlawed country sprawling across Eurasia, had become the heart of the largest, most predatory political and ideological empire ever known. Friendly neighbors indeed!

For Stalin yielded nothing. Indeed, neglecting his half-ruined country's crying need for internal reconstruction, he rejected Truman's generous if imprudent offer to "collectivize" the ultimate weapon and scraped from his nearly empty treasury enough billions not only to manufacture his own A- and H-bombs in record time but to embark upon an expensive project of creating rocket-propelled missiles (bigger models of the German wartime V-1 and V-2) upon which he could leapfrog America's superiority in conventional aviation.

Weak as he was, Stalin boldly burned his bridges to the West. On February 9, 1946, a month before Churchill spoke in Missouri, the Georgian made a declaration of Cold War that should have ended all further Western illusions of accommodation with the Soviets. He stated that a peaceful world order was "impossible under the present capitalist development of the economy." George Kennan, then chargé d'affaires in Moscow, reported that this meant further Soviet "power expansion" by a "political force committed fanatically to the belief that with the United States there can be no permanent modus vivendi, that it is desirable and necessary that our society be disrupted, our traditional way of life be destroyed, the international authority of our state be broken, if Soviet power is to be secure." Wasted effort.

Yet gradually Harry S. Truman was seeing the light. Previous optimistic reports from Moscow by Joseph E. Davies and Harry Hopkins, the hopeful outlook of Secretary of State Byrnes—these simply did not jibe with the visible facts. At the end of 1945 the Soviets were still stubbornly refusing to pull their troops out of Iran. Therefore, the American President on December 31, 1945, in a long talk with Byrnes, turned over a new political leaf. It was too late to recover East Europe. The best he and his tireless Secretary of State could get was a series of peace treaties that confirmed the Soviet-imposed armistice terms and established Communist-dominated governments which the United States somewhat ruefully recognized. But Truman could try hard to prevent further losses. After one last offer of a compromise on Germany, the United States ceased trying to appease the unappeaseable.

From then on, he sought to "get along with the Russians by being tough"—short of war. Not for nothing had he learned in World War One that the duty of an artillery captain was to die on the guns.

As a result, the next five years (1946 through 1950) were greatly creative. By a series of energetic acts, along a great arc from Spitzbergen to Iran, Truman repelled every Soviet thrust with the exception of that in Czechoslovakia, of which more anon. But the major achievements deserve listing.

Through the United Nations (a first success), he persuaded the Russians officially to withdraw their wartime garrison from Iran, and later encouraged the Iranian government to recover the semi-Communized province of Azerbaijan, in defiance of Soviet threats, from the Communist Tudeh separatists.

He enabled Turkey to oppose Soviet claims to joint control of the Dardanelles and to the cession of the districts of Kars and Ardahan, despite menacing Red divisions massed in Bulgaria. The

President emphasized his support by sending the battleship *Missouri* to Istanbul.

When the British could no longer stand the financial strain of saving Greece from native Communists, supported from Communist Yugoslavia and Albania, Truman acted. He persuaded Congress to vote the necessary money, sent General James A. Van Fleet and a skilled group of American military advisers, who helped the Greeks hold the line until Yugoslavia's defection from the Soviet bloc (though not from Communism) caused the rebellion in Greece to dry up for want of supplies.

When, in 1948, Tito (Josip Broz) broke with Stalin, Truman, in the teeth of considerable anti-Communism at home, gave the Yugoslavian enough aid to enable his "national Communism" to survive.

In Italy, twenty-one years of Fascist tragi-comedy had fostered the strongest Communist party in any Western country. In addition, Tito threatened to annex all Istria with Trieste and a strip along the Isonzo River. Truman beat off a Soviet bid for Italian Libya, and gave such intense support to the democratic Italian government that it weathered the meanest Communist offensive in the West, and eventually managed to reach a settlement with Yugoslavia that left Trieste on the Italian side.

France presented a different sort of problem. There, as in Italy, Communists had formed a great part of the internal resistance and guerrilla forces. They demanded and got a place in the first De Gaulle Cabinet and in several thereafter. They fanned the natural French fear of a resurgent Germany by contrasting the hard-fighting Stalin, "*père des peuples,*" with the inhuman Hitler. They supported De Gaulle's friendship treaty with the Soviet Union (December, 1944) and opposed every subsequent effort to bring France into an integrated West Europe that would include a re-armed (West) Germany. Yet gradually, under the influence of the Truman policies and their natural recovery, the French people eliminated Communists from the national government and greatly reduced their influence.

Early in his Presidential career, Truman singlehandedly, as we have seen, saved Britain by inducing Congress to grant it a huge loan. In 1947, by the Act of Rio de Janeiro, he took the United States into far closer relations with the Latin-American countries. A year later he gave quick diplomatic recognition to the new state of Israel, which was created by the U.N.'s decision to partition disputed Palestine.

All these were achievements. They were dwarfed, however, by Truman's five great steps that really saved Europe and certain other countries as well and constituted America's definitive recognition of its role as the leader of the West.

The first of these, stimulated by the need for aiding Greece and Turkey, was the "Truman doctrine" (March, 1947). This was the formalization by the Chief of State of the containment policy first put forth by George F. Kennan of the State Department. Kennan, an expert on Russia, had proposed that the United States "promote tendencies which must eventually find their outlet in either the mellowing or the break-up of Soviet power." The President emphasized the means:

"I believe," he told a joint session of Congress, "that it must be the policy of the United States to support free peoples who are resisting attempted subjugation by armed minorities or by outside pressure."

Truman followed this historical speech by a second constructive step, the Marshall Plan for post-war rehabilitation of European allies. This was outlined in two successive speeches by Under Secretary of State Dean Acheson and by Secretary of State George Marshall. To be sure, under pressure from incurably pro-Russian Americans, the Secretary first felt obliged to state that it was not directed against the Soviet Union, "but against hunger, poverty, desperation and chaos." Even after six years of Soviet trickery, many Americans (and perhaps more Europeans) were still unready to admit that Stalin had taken the dead Hitler's place as the chief enemy of mankind. And, above all, the country and its government were, as Forrestal put it, "desperately anxious to avoid war." Therefore, the offer originally included Communist-committed countries as recipients; the same mistake the United States made at the close of the war in the United Nations Relief and Rehabilitation Administration.

However, the Soviet Union rescued Marshall and Truman by scornfully refusing aid under the plan and compelling its rueful satellites, including Czechoslovakia and Poland, which had already accepted, to do likewise. In consequence, this plan put West Europe back on its feet and was the first step toward the coming Western Alliance.

Next Truman, in his 1949 Inaugural, announced his Point Four Program of technical assistance. It became law in 1950 as the Act for International Development. He hoped that by eliminating misery and want, the United States could prevent nations from succumbing to the siren yodeling of Communism. At the time of writing his *Memoirs* the President considered it "the strongest antidote to communism that has so far been put into practice." For the alternative was to "allow those vast areas to drift toward poverty, despair, fear and the other miseries of mankind that breed unending wars."

Truman's next and revolutionary achievement was the reunification and rehabilitation of West Germany. The four occupying powers had taken separate zones of occupation but had planned to administer Germany as a unit under lasting military surveillance, curbing any too rapid revival. Stalin broke the agreement, first by looting whatever his soldiers could reach in any zone, then by buying everything else available with worthless "occupation marks" which were printed from American plates. Moreover, he speedily established East Germany (later called the

German Democratic Republic) as a separate Communist satellite. This cost both the United States and Britain a lot of money, since they were unwilling to see even guilty Germans starve. Stalin did not mind.

Thanks to Stalin's faithlessness, it became clear to Truman and Marshall that to preserve the rest of Europe from Soviet subversion and aggression, Germany must be revived and morally rehabilitated. Once they saw that Stalin intended to have his way with Germany regardless of his allies or his previous agreements, the way was open for a drastic change. Machiavelli said that a wise victor should handle a powerful vanquished enemy in one of two ways: either by imposing a peace so drastic as to make future hostilities impossible or a peace so light as to permit reconciliation. As the Soviets gradually turned the original common policy against the Western powers, the latter started reviving their (reunited) sixty per cent of the country. They put through a currency reform that triggered what was to become the "German economic miracle" and started creating a unified and self-governing West Germany.

The Kremlin's answer to the Marshall Plan and the new anti-Communist West Germany was swift and twofold. Nine Communist governments met and decided to "defeat American imperialism." Next the Kremlin organized a take-over of Czechoslovakia, which had had the impudence to accept Marshall Plan aid and been stopped only by a Soviet veto. Soon thereafter, that Western-minded country became the most servile of Soviet satellites. The United States, which had sparked this trend by refusing to liberate Czechoslovakia in 1945, again missed a chance to intervene.

Russia next struck back by blockading West Berlin, access to which by the West had been ill-defined in the days of wartime camaraderie with Stalin. The idea was to starve two million West Berliners into accepting East German (really Soviet) rule.

Truman refused General Lucius Clay's proposal to break the

blockade on land by an armored train, if only because, as Secretary Forrestal reminded Marshall, the total American army reserve was down to about two and a third divisions. But the President prepared to resist possible Soviet violence with the A-bomb. And acting together with Britain, he frustrated the Russians with a gigantic airlift that proved able to satisfy indefinitely the needs of both the Allied garrisons and the West Berliners.

After a year, during which the West Berliners' patriotism rose to a high pitch, the Soviets offered peace on the basis of the preexisting situation. Truman accepted. Thereafter, the rehabilitation of the West German Republic went forward unhindered. Moreover, the President's political education was advancing. Three months before the Soviet grab of Czechoslovakia, Marshall had optimistically reported that the advance of Communism had been stemmed. Shortly after his victory at Berlin, Truman decided that the way to stop Communism while avoiding a third world war was to "stamp out the smouldering beginnings of any conflict" and lead from strength.

This was, at long last, American recognition of the Cold War which Stalin had declared in February, 1946.

In its long history Europe had known countless catastrophes. But World War Two did more to weaken it than anything since the Black Death in the Fourteenth Century. Industry, housing, communications and food production declined disastrously. Yet a revived and strong Europe was essential if Soviet expansion was to be stopped. Moreover, many on both sides of the Atlantic believed that in the age of giant states, Europe, recently the center of world civilization and power, must unite or cease to count. For the first time since June, 1940, when Churchill made his last-minute offer of union with France, the British Conservative Party seemed ready to recognize that whatever its former "world status," Britain's fate was thenceforth somewhat tied to that of the countries with which it shared a common history and civilization.

Schemes for various degrees of European integration multiplied.

The United States backed all such moves. Truman and his advisers wanted above all to restore West Europe's immunity against further Soviet encroachment or outright attack. For this purpose, they believed the restoration and rearmament of West Germany in some form to be essential.

This inevitably revived the memory of German aggression and awakened intense opposition in those peoples that had known and suffered from German invasion and occupations. Progress, therefore, was slow at first. An early plan, named for France's then Premier, René Pleven, was to create a single European Defense Community with a common army. But the British Labor Government was hostile to such close entanglement with the Continent and since Truman, acting on Eisenhower's advice, agreed to leave British as well as American forces out of this European force, France found the prospect of being ultimately dominated by a rearmed West Germany unpalatable. Nonetheless, Truman, aided at home by Senator Arthur Vandenberg and in Britain by Prime Minister Attlee, laid the foundation for the first peacetime military alliance in American history. Eventually a way was found to unite forces from the eventual fifteen member states without completely merging them.

The American author of such daring policies had reason to be proud of them. Particularly because, in order to carry them out he had both to get himself re-elected (1948) and at the same time to meet and overcome a recrudescence of pacifist and pro-Soviet feeling at home.

During the campaign, the perspicacious Forrestal commented that "the most dangerous spot is our own country because the people are so eager for peace and have such a distaste for war that they . . . grasp for any sign of a solution of a problem that has . . . them worried." Fervent admirers of F.D.R. like his son Elliott and former Vice President Henry Wallace accused the peace-minded Truman of provoking the Soviets and were backed by what Truman described as well-meaning groups who "campaigned for peace at any price while apologizing for the aggressive acts of the Russians."

Nonetheless, the President from Independence, Missouri, though occasionally making a conciliatory gesture in the direction of these groups, resolutely transformed an American policy of peacetime isolation that dated from George Washington into permanent world participation. Moreover, by persuading Congress to establish the Central Intelligence Agency and the National Security Council, he sought to streamline the Administration for the task of world leadership. His request for universal military training, though unsuccessful, was a further effort in this direction. By his courageous innovations he achieved a distinguished place in history. Yet his fame would have been greater but for his blank misunderstanding of the importance in world affairs of the new Far East.

Chapter VI

DISASTER IN THE FAR EAST

> "Edgar, you know next to nothing about China."
>
> "You obviously know even less about communism, John."
>
> (From a discussion between John Carter Vincent, Director of Far Eastern Office, U.S. State Department, and the author, in November, 1945)

Nothing in American history quite equals the complacency with which high U.S. officials, beginning with Harry S. Truman, accepted the Communization of China. Many of those who, in 1960, were pointing to Red China as the "chief enemy," from which we should seek to detach "revisionist" Russia, were saying in the late Forties that nothing—repeat, nothing—that might happen in the Far East for many years ahead could endanger America.

Yet, although Truman was President when China went Red, it was not entirely his fault. He had inherited from his predecessor a theory that, while already demonstrably unsound in East Europe, he felt obliged to continue applying in the Far East. This was that Communists would cooperate "honorably" with non-Communists. Truman followed this policy both in China and

Korea (though not, fortunately, in Japan and the Philippines) until it blew up in his face. Yet while allowing Communism to take over China and refusing to reunite divided Korea by fighting Red China, he hotly repudiated any accusation of appeasement. His later explanation was that to have followed another course would, or might, have led straight to a third world war. Yet a similar repugnance to risk World War Two at Munich in 1938 brought upon Prime Minister Chamberlain and Premier Daladier an almost worldwide charge of appeasing Hitler.

Nor did Truman appear to have suspected that an American policy of pure defense against an aggressor was more likely to lead to the war he feared than one of resolute counteroffensive. Yet it is only fair to stress that both in advocating cooperation with Communists and in refraining from provoking Communist aggressors, he was only continuing what had been the policy of his predecessor in the White House, and was to become the policy of his successor.

At Cairo in November, 1943, F.D.R., after a first meeting with Chiang Kai-shek, complained that the latter was "keeping thousands and thousands of his best men" containing Chinese Communists instead of fighting the Japanese. And he further informed son Elliott that he had told Chiang "that he would have to form a unity government, while the war was still being fought, with the Communists in Yenan. And Chiang agreed. In return, the President continued, "we will support his contention that the British and other nations no longer enjoy special Empire rights to Hong Kong, Shanghai and Canton."

What Truman did thereafter was simply to insist on Chiang's living up to his Cairo promise to F.D.R. and forming what the latter had labeled a "more democratic government."

One may ask why Truman, who by the end of 1945 had seen through Stalin's deceptive "democracy" in East Europe, should have clung to Roosevelt's illusion in China. For of all the Communist parties in the world, China's was the closest to Russia. In fact until the Russian revolution, there was no hint of Communism in China. But Sun Yat-sen, the father of modern China, was a revolutionary and saw no good reason to bar from his ruling Kuomintang the early Chinese converts to Marxism-Leninism. Moreover, after 1919, many modern-minded Chinese were bitterly disappointed with Western support of Japan's imperialistic claims upon China at Versailles and were inclined to look favorably upon the vociferous "anti-imperialists" in the Kremlin. Both Sun and Chiang welcomed Soviet advisers and worked with them for years. Chiang did not turn against the Communist "wing" of his ruling party until his northern expedition in the late Twenties to drive out the war lords and unify the divided country. At that time the Chinese Communists rebelled and, with Soviet and other Communist advisers egging them on, sought to take full power.

It took Chiang five separate military campaigns to defeat the Soviet converts in his country and to pen up the remnant of their armed forces in remote Shensi. But, underestimating their determination and alienation from the Chinese tradition, he did not seek to exterminate them or preach a crusade against their doctrines.

Neither Chiang Kai-shek nor many other leading Chinese realized that Communism was doing to its addicts what nothing in Chinese history had ever before accomplished—*sustaining a mood of fanaticism which had been previously demonstrated by the Boxers and the Taipings.*

Dr. Sun and his friends had sought the drastic modernization of China, but as an extension of ancient and respected Chinese attitudes and ethics, not in opposition to them. Among the first was devotion to China. Among the second was a humanitarianism and Confucian urbanity that favored compromise. Whatever their faults, no matter how sporadically cruel, few Chinese had been extremists. But Chinese Communists were fanatical followers of an un-Chinese philosophy. Marxism-Leninism transformed a deep resentment of national decadence and foreign encroachment into an inflexible ruthlessness. Chinese Communists became essentially like Communists everywhere.

This even Chiang, as he confessed in his book, *Soviet Russia in China,* was slow in understanding.

If the Chinese Communists and their sponsoring Soviet confederates could deceive their countrymen, small wonder that they were able to spread abroad a smoke screen that led not only Presidents Roosevelt and Truman but millions of non-Communists all over the world to sympathize with the Red plotters of Yenan. All Communists understood that the Chinese revolution was not only an integral part of the general revolution but, after success in Russia, the essential next step to Communist world dominion. But Moscow and Yenan spread the contrary notions: Chinese Communists were agrarian reformers without affiliation to Moscow; Communists everywhere were anti-imperialists; Japan was the Nazi Germany of the Far East and the United States could only gain by joining China and the Soviet Union in stopping that country.

Nowhere was this deliberate deception more widespread or successful than in the United States. More or less affiliated with the Institute of Pacific Relations, a dozen "pink" organizations strove to convince innocent anti-Fascist Americans that, whatever they thought of the U.S.S.R. (and thanks to the Depression some were not unfavorable), the Chinese Communists were different. Natalie Grant stated in her study, *Bear and Dragon,* that "over a period of twenty-five years (1925-1950), about five thousand persons worked, deliberately or as dupes, at supplying false information concerning Asia and Soviet Asian policy to the American people and inspiring views desirable to the Soviet Union." Communist Chinese leaders like Chou En-lai successfully pulled the wool over the eyes of Harry Hopkins, Wendell Willkie, Ambassador Pat

Hurley (for a while), Donald M. Nelson, Henry Wallace and even Averell Harriman.

Yet perhaps the greatest Communist propagandist of all was Chiang Kai-shek's own sister-in-law, Madame Sun Yat-sen, the revered widow of the father of the new China and founder of the Kuomintang.

Even today it is difficult to persuade Chinese Nationalists on Formosa, her victims, to say anything derogatory of this lady. Yet for many years Ching-ling (Happy Age) Sun lived in alleged retirement in a small Hong Kong apartment as the agent of the Chinese Communists. She later openly joined them.

Small, dignified, wrapped in the prestige of her husband, this unshakable leftist made it her business to influence visitors to China. Her line was simple: the Kuomintang was reactionary, if not Fascist. Chinese Communists, on the other hand, were democrats and deserved foreign liberal support. The Soviet Union had been an inspiration to her dead husband and was a great force for humanity and progress. (When, in the course of a conversation in Hong Kong in 1938, I ventured to demur, she went hard and treated me as a "reactionary.") Certain Americans who knew China best considered later that this dainty widow did more to help Chinese Communism abroad than any other Chinese.

In any event, the Chinese Reds did an unequaled job of bamboozling not only millions of Chinese but American writers, high-ranking officers and diplomats.

Basic to the situation was Japan's ambition to conquer China. This offensive started in 1931 and continued until Japan's surrender in September, 1945. Like its Fascist confederates in Europe, Japan at first followed "artichoke" tactics, pulling leaf by leaf from the body of China. The first leaf was Manchuria.

Chiang, compelled to fight a two-front war against the Japanese and the local Communists, was ineffective against both. In consequence, Communists and their Western liberal friends accused him of being "subservient to Japan." Yet at the same time, the Soviet Union not only concluded a neutrality pact with Japan (1941) but, according to Chiang, agreed on a second pact to divide China. Far better for him and perhaps for China (though not for the United States or the West) if he had been "subservient to Japan." For during ten good years Chiang could, like the one-time Chinese revolutionary, Wang Ching-wei, have secured a respectable position as a puppet of Japan. What Chiang did was move cautiously against Japan while isolating the Communist rebels.

The latter, by quick exploitation of a fortuitous situation, had finally induced Chiang to sign with them the Pact of Sian for a common front against the aggressor. The "Anti-Japanese People's United Front" theoretically put the Communist forces under Chiang's command. Actually, it restored their respectability and removed the cork from the bottle in Yenan, where Chiang had been pretty successfully keeping them. Naturally, the Communists used their freedom of action, not to fight the Japanese, but to infiltrate the countryside and ultimately, with Soviet help, to seize the entire country.

From 1937 until December, 1941, China's resistance to Japan seemed almost hopeless. After 1939, West Europe, intent on limiting the struggle against Hitler (the Phony War), had neither the strength nor the will to help China whose government simply "hung on and waited for a break."

Unhappily, this was not enough. The Chinese Nationalists, whose forces showed less initiative and combat readiness than their supposed Communist subordinates (who were actually deadly rivals) were almost bound to lag behind both in popular appeal and, when the time came, in making the most of a favorable situation. Nor could the Nationalists persuade the representatives of friendly countries that since they were doing the very best they could, they were deserving of full support.

To be sure, Pearl Harbor looked like salvation. Americans, beginning with President Roosevelt, were sincere friends. The United States had steadfastly insisted on the "open door" policy as a brake on further European encroachment. President Roosevelt envisaged a "strong, united and democratic China" as one of the four pillars of world order within his Great Design. He resisted Churchill's efforts to play down the Chinese potential. In fact, F.D.R. foresaw that, granted time and unity, China would again become a great power.

Had the United States been able to swing its full weight against Japan immediately after Pearl Harbor, China's history would have been happier. But the need for first defeating Hitler (which most American generals and political leaders insisted on) made it incumbent on already groggy China to hold on for almost four years more.

In sober fact, Pearl Harbor gave China to Communism by placing China's fate in the hands of one American President, F.D.R., who saw little or no reason to fear Communist expansion, and of a second, Truman, who would neither provoke the U.S.S.R. nor run the risk of major war (as he thought) by aiding the "undemocratic and incompetent regime" of Chiang Kai-shek.

In that decision, Truman had plenty of American backing. Almost from their first contacts with wartime China, some Americans disapproved of what they saw. During this period Americans in China divided roughly into three groups:

First, honest souls who knew little or nothing of Chinese history or of the awful confusion from which Chiang had all too slowly rescued most of his country or of the Communists' determination to take over the country by perpetuating that confusion. Instead, these honest souls were appalled at the poverty, corruption and police tyranny of Chiang's wartime administration.

Second, American officers who had expected to find a Western-type army in China and were deeply disturbed by Chiang's insistence on using some of his none too effective forces to watch his Communists rather than to fight the Japanese.

Third, American diplomats, many of them young reformers, who came to admire the Communists for their Spartan lives, discipline, wooing of the peasants (although they murdered anti-Communists as "collaborators" with Japan), and feeling for "democracy."

In their reports these diplomats hammered on two points: that Chiang's insistence on containing his Communists was militarily harmful to the United States; and that the Communists were winning over the people and would triumph over Chiang in the end unless he came to terms with them.

Clarence E. Gauss, Ambassador to China (1941-44), had no great opinion of Chiang, and General Joseph Stilwell, the ranking U.S. officer in the China-Burma-India theater of war until 1944, had only contempt for him. Stilwell feared that Chiang would attack the Communists, who were spreading their rule over unoccupied sections of China thanks to their carefully planned division of effort—"70 per cent expansion, 20 per cent against the government, 10 per cent against the Japanese."

When finally in answer to Stilwell's demand that the Kuomintang permit Americans to arm and lead the Communists, Chiang insisted on having Stilwell replaced, President Roosevelt and General Marshall took that insistence badly.

Stilwell's replacement, General Albert C. Wedemeyer, and General Claire Chennault, the air commander, understood Chiang's problems. But their voices were stilled by the drumfire of official and unofficial American criticism. In July, 1943, in the *Far Eastern Survey*, published by the Institute of Pacific Relations, T. A. Bisson coolly spoke of "two Chinas"—one "feudalistic" (under the National Government) and the other "democratic" (under the Communists). And by 1945 a large number of Americans (and perhaps most Europeans) were convinced that nothing but

Chiang's "reactionary clique" prevented Nationalists and Communists from harmoniously cooperating in military and political fields to win the war and together restore the country.

This was the background against which F.D.R. went to Yalta and bartered away Chinese control of Manchuria in exchange for Stalin's promise to help beat the Japanese and to support, not the "margarine communists" (his own expression) in China, but the National Government—provided of course that it cooperated with Stalin's little friend, Mao Tse-tung.

Apologists for F.D.R. have argued both that Soviet participation in the war against Japan was necessary to "save American lives" (General Douglas MacArthur wanted no less than sixty Soviet divisions) and that the National Government "freely accepted" the Yalta terms. Actually, Chiang accepted the Yalta decisions as enlarged and confirmed at Moscow only because he could do nothing else, as I learned from Foreign Minister T. V. Soong shortly after his Moscow visit. Soong resigned rather than sign the only agreement he could get.

Fourteen years of continuous warfare had left ravages that made Chiang completely dependent upon outside help. Nonetheless he refused Stalin's suggestion that China become "nonaligned," reluctantly abided by Roosevelt's agreement with Stalin, and hoped for the best.

He could do nothing else. During the war China had mobilized some fourteen million men and suffered over three million casualties. It spent several billion U.S. dollars. Its railroads were a wreck, its scanty industry disorganized. To provide airfields and roads for American forces, and support even scantily its hungry population, the government had printed money recklessly. Both the technical ability and authority of its government were less than in devastated Europe. The recovery of more developed Manchuria might have helped, but the Soviet "liberators" stripped that territory of machinery and plant valued by Edwin W. Pauley at eight hundred and fifty million dollars and with a replacement cost of two billion. The Soviets then turned over the remainder, along with the surrendered Japanese arms, to their Communist allies. As the war drew to an end, Communist commanders followed up the retreating Japanese and occupied 300,000 square miles of territory with some ninety million people.

As a result, conditions remained chaotic in the territories the Nationalist armies reoccupied, while Communists and Russians prevented full revival of communications and access to other important areas. Yet Americans like Theodore H. White and Annalee Jacoby blamed the Kuomintang for the disorder and urged "a new and united government" since a China remaining under the Kuomintang alone would, in their eyes, be a "historical monstrosity."

President Truman agreed. He had been amply warned, by trusted advisers like Averell Harriman and George F. Kennan, among others, not to count on Soviet support of American objectives in China. But he had Chiang's pledge to F.D.R. to cooperate with his Communists and Stalin's promise to give all aid solely to the Nationalists as the only government of China. The thing was for Chiang to get busy and produce a "free, united and democratic government." So Ambassador Hurley induced Chiang to appoint a Communist as one of China's delegates to the San Francisco Conference! In exchange, the Americans were in theory prepared to help Chiang's troops reoccupy all of his country. But in practice, when these movements were blocked by Communist forces or Russian vetos (as at Dairen), the American forces simply withdrew. General Wedemeyer suggested that the United States should give more help to Chiang (he asked for seven American divisions) or get out. So, in November, 1945, did Secretary of the Navy Forrestal.

Truman and Marshall felt that the United States could hardly give Chiang sufficient military help to win and, furthermore, that it should not do so lest it offend the U.S.S.R. Above all, they feared direct Soviet intervention in a Chinese civil war. An alternative, they insisted, was bringing the two rival claimants to China together.

Yet however attractive in principle, such an undertaking was impractical, as a far-sighted few warned at the time. For on what terms could Chinese Nationalists and Communists unite? Chiang would accept unity only if the Communists entered *his* government shorn of all powers they might later use to overthrow it. Mao would "cooperate" with Chiang only in a sort of popular front like those which the U.S.S.R. had used in East Europe as steppingstones to Communist take-over. Meanwhile, Mao simply refused to attend the National Assembly convoked by Chiang, lest attendance cramp continued Communist expansion.

Shortly before the Postdam meeting (July-August, 1945), Truman formally ordered the American armed forces in China *not* to support Chiang in a civil war. In September, 1945, he told T. V. Soong in Washington that American military assistance should not be "diverted for use in fratricidal warfare or to support undemocratic administrations." At the end of that year, it was made clear to General Wedemeyer that while he was to help the Nationalists get the Japanese out of China, he was *not* to support the National Government directly against the Communists. In November Secretary Byrnes suggested telling Chiang that the United States would stop essential aid to his government unless he compromised with Mao. Byrnes thought that attempted intervention between the Chinese "factions" was "like trying to intervene between a married couple."

And from the end of hostilities until the end of 1946, Communist tactics were masterly. They consisted in blocking the Nationalists locally by force of arms, occupying as much other territory as possible, avoiding decisive battle and showing just enough willingness to negotiate to discourage Chiang from the all-out effort to crush them which might, many thought, have succeeded. (When Chiang did finally try to destroy his enemy, Truman reproached him for "attempting to settle major social issues by resort to force.")

Meanwhile the U.S.S.R. had legal title for the fictitious independence of an Outer Mongolia which it had held for a generation. From there it organized and supported with air power a Mongolian force that invaded Sinkiang, where there were no Japanese.

By November, 1945, Chiang's position had not improved. He had not restored satisfactory conditions in the areas he had reoccupied. Communists were appearing in ever more localities and systematically cutting communications between others. Soviet troops were still lingering in Manchuria and impeding Chiang's efforts to establish himself firmly there. The Chinese people were sick of war and the Communists promised food, shelter and peace. Even more of the people were deciding that the Generalissimo had "lost the mandate of heaven," a death sentence for a Chinese regime. Worse, the crash demobilization in the United States had so debilitated American strength that President Truman concluded that "we could not send in the kind of force that could ensure that Chiang would prevail." If this were true, the President's alternatives were either to do nothing and let nature take its course; or to supply Chiang abundantly with American war matériel and leave the outcome to him; or to stick to F.D.R.'s original policy of forcing Nationalists and Communists to reach a peaceful settlement.

Truman chose the last. To engineer this obviously difficult feat, he picked as "mediator" the man he considered the "greatest living American." If General George C. Marshall could not do the trick, nobody could.

Unhappily, the Marshall mission was foredoomed to failure, for its purpose was to give Communism a share in governing China without letting it usurp total rule. *But this was asking Communists to cease being what they were.* To make matters worse, Marshall was to wield over Chiang alone a bludgeon: no further help without Chinese unity.

The President's directive (whose real authorship has never been revealed) to General Marshall was in fact an ultimatum to Chiang Kai-shek: cease fighting the Communists or the United States will wash its hands of you. Truman himself made this clear, as well as his *idée fixe* that "the various elements in China could be persuaded to unify the country." In that famous directive, the President said:

"You [Marshall] may state [to Chiang] that a China disunited and torn by civil strife would not be considered realistically as a proper place for American assistance." Further that "National Government troops will not be transported by the United States into areas such as North China where their introduction would prejudice [sic] the objectives of the military truce and the political negotiations."

China, Truman said, "had a clear responsibility to eliminate a conflict within its territory as constituting a threat to world peace." On the other hand, the directive's key sentence ran: "As China *moves toward peace and unity* the United States would be prepared to assist the national Government in every *reasonable* way to rehabilitate the country, improve the agrarian and industrial economy and establish a military organization capable of discharging Chinese national and international responsibilities for the maintenance of peace and order." (My italics.)

Such a directive was self-defeating. To Mao it said that to prevent American aid to Chiang, he need only raise his terms high enough to make them unacceptable, thus stopping any move toward "peace and unity." This is exactly what Mao did. Yet since Chiang must have doubted his own ability to survive without American help, he had no alternative but to try to win that aid by negotiating. In the process he squandered the year the Marshall mission lasted (roughly all of 1946) during which by a supreme military offensive he might perhaps have destroyed his enemies.

Marshall tried hard. He went to China. He persistently brought the two sides together. He cajoled and he scolded. He once interrupted his futile labors and returned home to report. He threatened to break off altogether unless the two sides became "reasonable." And all the time he urged Truman to "clear our hands out here as quickly as possible in order to avoid the inevitable Soviet recriminations." He was embarrassed by the Red claim that the United States had aided Chiang in retaking Changchun, and compelled Chiang to suspend operations there.

He also induced Truman to cancel the appointment as Ambassador to China of General Wedemeyer (Hurley had resigned, angrily charging lack of support in upholding the National Government and disloyalty in his pro-Mao subordinates) lest the appearance of the pro-Chinese Wedemeyer upset his current "delicate negotiations" with the Chinese Communists.

True to his threat, Truman began to cut back American military supplies to Chiang and withhold military advice. The American Treasury, perhaps influenced by the pro-Russians Harry Dexter White, Frank Coe and Lauchlin Currie, refused to make a new large loan to China.

Finally, in January, 1947, Marshall threw in the sponge, went home and washed his hands of the struggle. He still blamed his failure, not on the impossibility of his task, but on "extremists on both sides" and chiefly on Chiang. Truman and he saw the Chinese issue, not as a death struggle between two incompatible societies, but as one between "adamant Communism on one side and unyielding reaction on the other."

Thereafter, American aid to National China was negligible. The President rewarded his favorite general by making him Secretary of State. Both men were obviously resigned to a Communist victory. Yet they never actually said so. Marshall, however, expected Chiang to lose, considering his armies overextended. Dean Acheson, then Under Secretary of State, saw no connection between the Yalta agreements bringing Russia into China and Chiang's defeat which, as late as March, 1947, he did not consider imminent.

By 1947, however, Chiang's plight was disturbing many Americans, including members of the Republican Eightieth Congress, later so persistently denounced as "do-nothing" by Truman. They were ready to give massive aid to National China. But by this time, Truman and Marshall, now Secretary of State, were directing most of their energies to saving Europe. The last thing they wanted was to let public opinion concentrate on their failure to relieve Chiang. To be sure, Truman had by this time adopted "containment" as the official U.S. policy and backed it by the Truman Doctrine. Republicans at home and the Chinese government asked that the doctrine be immediately applied to National China. They asked, why save Greece from Communism and write off a more important country?

To mollify those whom they called the "China Lobby" (overlooking the pro-Communist lobby, which was going strong), Truman and Marshall asked General Wedemeyer, as a known partisan of Chiang, to return to China and report on the situation. Chiang still had about three million soldiers to half that many Communists.

How far Truman and Marshall foresaw what happened is not clear. There were no strings on Wedemeyer. He wrote his own directive. But while in China, at the suggestion of the new U.S. Ambassador, Leighton Stuart, Wedemeyer made a public speech strongly criticizing the Generalissimo for the all too obvious "maladministration, corruption and lethargy" of the regime.

Not content with this, the general released a statement even more critical of the people he wished to help. Both his speech and his statement received broad publicity, further convincing many Americans that any substantial help given to Chiang would be wasted.

This was exactly what Wedemeyer did not think. In his formal report he recommended giving large-scale "moral, advisory and military support to China." But he reckoned without Marshall, whose judgment was gold to Truman. On the pretext that Wedemeyer's further recommendation that the United States seek to preserve Manchuria by putting it under a United Nations trusteeship might offend the Chinese, Marshall coolly suppressed the report and kept it from the knowledge of the Republican Congress for two whole years. Thus instead of helping China, Wedemeyer all unintentionally damaged that country.

True, all during 1948, by which time Ambassador Stuart was also recommending help, Congress repeatedly voted money for China aid. Even Truman once asked for funds. But next to nothing ever reached Chiang. Munition shortages further demoralized his badly scattered forces. Finally, Chiang's generals started surrendering, or rather, deserting, to Communist generals, handing over what matériel they possessed, some of it American. This fact the Administration largely publicized. It ignored further appeals from Chiang.

In October, 1949, victorious Communists at Peiping proclaimed the People's Republic of China, with Mao and Chou naturally taking the top jobs. Another of Lenin's great ambitions was fulfilled. In December, a few thousand Nationalists escaped to Formosa and set up a new capital at Taipei, preceded by Chiang who had resigned as President somewhat earlier.

Truman was not dismayed. Although he refrained from following trade-hungry Britain and a few other non-Communist states in recognizing Red China, he wrote National China off. Chiang had not "reformed" and it served him right. The United States was not responsible. To prove it, he and the Secretary of State published a thick diplomatic White Paper (July, 1949). The key sentences were: "The unfortunate but inescapable fact is that the ominous result of the civil war in China was beyond the control of the government of the United States. Nothing that this country did or could have done within the reasonable limits of its capabilities could have changed that result. Nothing that was left undone by this country has contributed to it." But where were the "reasonable limits"? American opinions differed sharply.

Secretary of State Acheson further anticipated the speedy fall of Formosa and strove to cushion the shock to the public by stating in advance that it had little or no strategic value. When some in Congress proposed that the United States should occupy and defend that island, Truman publicly stated that the United States had no intention either of establishing bases or of providing "military aid or advice" to the Chinese forces there.

To make the Administration's meaning doubly clear, Secretary Acheson omitted Formosa and Korea from the "areas of strength" which the United States publicly undertook to defend, leaving their defense to the United Nations. The Secretary hoped Mao would turn Titoist. Acheson sought good relations with Communist China, intended to build up Japan and was taking no chances of antagonism from Mao. Almost while he was speaking, Red Russia and Red China signed a treaty of alliance. But neither the Democratic Eighty-first Congress nor the American people were too disturbed by that.[1]

Their awakening was swift. Less than half a year later, North Korean Communists invaded South Korea and within a few days a United States that had refused to risk a fight to save half a

[1] George F. Kennan, then a senior State Department official, stated in October, 1949, "The Russians are perhaps the people least able to combine with the Chinese in developing the resources of China and producing anything which in a physical sense would be dangerous to us."

billion people from Communism was shedding its blood to preserve the tip of a small Asian peninsula.

The basic facts are well known. Soviet forces that had in 1945 divided Korea with Americans, refused to fulfill their promise of uniting the country, Communized their area, and proceeded to arm it heavily. Meanwhile, the United States, embarrassed by its half of the burden, set it up as the Republic of Korea (under the veteran patriot, Syngman Rhee), withdrew American troops, and placed the new state under the protection of the United Nations.

In June, 1950, North Korean tanks and heavy artillery, with Soviet advisers and Soviet planes, tore through the poorly armed South Koreans and soon were well on the way to "uniting" the peninsula under Moscow and Peiping. Truman, with characteristic courage and energy, convoked the United Nations and got, in the absence of the Soviet Union from the Security Council meeting, a declaration of aggression and a decision to intervene. Even while the U.N. was debating, he ordered General MacArthur in Japan to save the Republic of Korea. He further reversed his previous position and ordered the Seventh Fleet to defend Formosa. Both acted effectively. MacArthur held an entrenched camp in Pusan in the south until he could land an amphibious force behind the North Koreans on the west coast. He captured many, and the rest withdrew to somewhere near their original positions. South Korea was saved. What next?

The response of other members of the United Nations was uneven. Ultimately, fifteen in addition to the United States made military contributions, some of them excellent. They supplied about 40,000 combatants as against 500,000 South Koreans and 400,000 Americans and suffered four per cent of the casualties. They also insisted on influencing the campaign. Thanks in part to them, the U.N. refused the assistance of 33,000 Nationalist Chinese offered by Chiang—allegedly lest their departure weaken the defenses of Formosa, but actually because the U.N. members, including the United States, were fearful of "provoking" the Chinese Communists.

In October, the U.N. General Assembly passed a resolution reiterating the objective of a "unified, independent and democratic Korea." MacArthur launched a general offensive to win the war and by November had almost reached the Manchurian border. Shortly thereafter "unprovoked" Red Chinese armies, 850,000 strong, that had presumably been prepared for an assault on Formosa but were deterred by Truman's shift of policy, launched a massive counteroffensive against the overextended MacArthur and, fighting better than any Chinese had fought since the defense of Shanghai against Japan, threw the United Nations forces back behind the frontier and again occupied Seoul, the South Korean capital. MacArthur called this "an entirely new war," and asked for permission to carry hostilities into China itself.

Then Truman made the remark that changed everything. In the course of a press confrence, he told an inquiring reporter that, if necessary, he might use the atom bomb. There were no strategical or ethical reasons why he should not do so if its use against Japan had been justified, as Truman thought. There were obvious psychological and political reasons. The Asian nations had always been hostile to Western intervention in the Far East. And Prime Minister Attlee of Britain chose to believe that, since the Soviets had exploded their own atom bomb a year before, any use of it against Red China might start an atomic world war. Furthermore, Attlee thought he could persuade Red China that its "real friends" were in London and Washington (and thereby save defenseless Hong Kong). He scurried to Washington and after three days of intense argument convinced Truman that it would be better to stop the war, leaving Korea as divided as before, than take a chance of Russia's coming to the aid of its Chinese ally. U.S.

officials insisted that there existed a "broad basis for settlement in Korea." Five other countries agreed.

The United Nations appointed a Good Offices Committee, which had "no remote interest in victory," and Truman decided to conduct a limited war until the Red Chinese leaders accepted reasonable terms. MacArthur was dismissed for airing contrary views in a public statement to Congressman Joe Martin. The Senate later held exhaustive hearings on the MacArthur dismissal and reviewed the whole Far Eastern affair. MacArthur and Wedemeyer urged a blockade of Red China. Acheson and Marshall defended the wisdom of not extending hostilities lest we "lose our European allies." General Bradley declared any such hostilities would "have been the wrong war, at the wrong time, and in the wrong place."

The Red Chinese refused to sign an armistice with the American "paper tiger" until, two years later, President Eisenhower threatened the use of atom bombs if they did not sign. Even then, they refused to return a certain number of American prisoners and consistently acted like victors.

Presumably they were. Although Acheson and others claimed that in successfully defending South Korea, the U.N. had accomplished its original purpose, the record showed that the U.N.'s declared goal of uniting Korea had not been reached. General Wedemeyer sourly commented that the Communist third team had tied the American first team. General MacArthur believed that there was no substitute for victory—that failure to win in Asia would mean the eventual loss of Europe. The veteran French general, Jean de Lattre de Tassigny, accepted the command of French troops in Indo-China because he was convinced that Europe could best be defended there. Many Americans still failed to understand why saving Greece and Turkey was more important than saving China and uniting Korea.

General Marshall answered that it was less dangerous. He believed that Russia would not fight to seize West Europe but would defend its Chinese ally from defeat. Averell Harriman complained that MacArthur had "a strange idea that we should back anybody who will fight Communism." Truman himself called MacArthur's desire to free China a "policy of aggression."

Even after all the hearings, some basic questions remained unanswered: Could and, if so, should, the United States have saved China from Communism even at the risk of atomic war with Russia (if risk there was, for the Soviets had exploded their first atom bomb only in 1949)? Or, having failed to save China, should the United Nations have reunited Korea by force? And further, should the United States have taken Red China's intervention in Korea as a useful pretext for crushing the Chinese Reds and restoring Chiang to the mainland? Thoughtful Americans are still divided on these points, and doubtless will remain so until history gives the formal reply.

But if the questions are unanswered, certain facts are beyond discussion. First, there would have been no Korean war if the United States had saved National China. Second, there might have been no Communist North Vietnam, no Laos and Cambodia tottering on the edge of ruin had the United Nations united Korea by force ten years earlier. Third, success in Korea made Red China a great military power, conceivably a graver danger than Red Russia. The historian Jules Davids, after a judicious defense of Truman's Far Eastern policies, admitted that "Korea was a setback—the first of a series of setbacks which took place during the 1950's!"

Truman argued that such facts became visible only through hindsight. Certainly most Americans were happy to avoid war with Red China and welcomed the inconclusive Korean armistice. But other Americans did foresee approximately what happened later. And in any case, American opinion notwithstanding, ignorance is no excuse for error.

> *"Inexorable is history. It makes*
> *No count of how well-meant were our mistakes."*
> (Paul Scott Mowrer)

The first duty of national leaders is to be right. It would be an irony if the Korean war turned out to be "the wrong war, at the wrong time, and in the wrong place" only because that war should have been fought in China some years earlier. If so, the responsibility was Truman's. From New Year's Day, 1946, his policy had been *stopping Communism without major war.*

Significantly, each time he followed his own Doctrine and fearlessly aided peoples struggling against Communist aggression or subversion, he succeeded. Where he sought primarily to avoid major war, he either failed to stop Communism or checked it only temporarily. And when, as with China, he simply ignored the Doctrine, he failed tragically—and all free men with him.

Chapter VII

EISENHOWER'S BOLD NEW PROGRAM

"It is no doubt a good thing to conquer but it takes greater wisdom and greater skill to make use of victory."

—POLYBIUS

In November, 1952, a solid majority of American voters turned the Democrats out of the White House after twenty years and brought in the victorious war hero, General Dwight D. Eisenhower. The Republicans had picked him because he seemed a winner and the people wanted a change. Republican sloganeers translated this wish into an attack on three "soft" spots in the Truman record—"corruption, Communism and Korea."

On the first point, the Democrats were only "normally" vulnerable. In political morality Americans, regardless of party, have never ranked higher than some of the peoples whose alleged "corruption" they love to criticize.

Unquestionably, the Democratic regime had been slow to remove from office and position Communists and pro-Communists who had wormed their way in during the New Deal and the Soviet-American partnership against Hitler.

Yet the Korean issue was perhaps the best the Republicans had. Despite his renunciation of further attempts to reunite that country, Truman found himself unable to obtain satisfactory truce terms from the Chinese Reds, and was obliged to continue fighting a demoralizing defensive struggle.

This was something the American people had never done before and did not relish. The war in Korea was not popular. An Administration that did not consider a Soviet-Chinese combination in the Far East to be a serious threat to the United States had failed to awaken popular enthusiasm for the abstract principle of collective action against aggression. The Republican platform charged that the Democrats "had waged the war in Korea without the will to victory and by their hampering orders produced stalemates and ignominious bartering with our enemies."

President Eisenhower's campaign promise to visit Korea ("I shall make that trip"), implying that he would bring to an end the "dissipation of American resources in a remote indecisive struggle," practically assured his election.

But however reluctant to die in "Truman's war"—that is, fighting Chinese Communists on a static line that left Korea divided—a majority of Americans were more disturbed by the progress of Communism in Asia than the Democratic leaders seemed to be. Thus in May, 1951, General Albert C. Wedemeyer, who had wanted an American effort to save National China, stated:

"I travel the length and breadth of this land and I talk with filling station attendants, coal miners, businessmen, bankers, farmers, ranchers—and they are solid. . . . All they want is a fearless leadership."

This seemed to fit Eisenhower. Truman and Acheson appeared to be seeking nothing more than a better position from which to bargain. The general promised more—something many took to mean putting an end to the Soviet threat. In an early election speech, he set forth his policy. Excluding both "appeasement" and a "stupidly aggressive attitude," he outlined his own choice:

"The third course is to prosecute the Cold War . . . with vigor and wisdom. . . . The prerequisite of . . . victory is a single-minded determination to get the job done."

Victory, mind you, nothing less—not "containment" or the modus vivendi with Communism of which he was later to become so fond.

Eisenhower's Secretary of State-designate, John Foster Dulles, with whom he worked in complete trust and confidence, had in 1950 set forth the foundation for a "bold new program" in his book, *War or Peace*. This was a belief that under the pressure of faith and hope and peaceful works, the rigid, topheavy and over-extended structure of Communist rule would come into a state of collapse.

To apply such pressure meant launching a "counteroffensive" against godless Communism by all means short of war. In Dulles' eyes, Communism was a "system of evil" and so dangerous that all other dangers threatening human freedom were secondary. Since it was evil, people would never acquiesce in it. Hence, under pressure of steady opposition limiting its expansion and rigid deterrence to aggression, it must ultimately collapse of its own inherent weaknesses. The "bold new program" was a policy of liberation.

It was not, however, a policy of "rollback" by force, as its adversaries proclaimed. Eisenhower personally had the word "retaliation" removed from the Republican platform. He sought somehow to combine Dulles' "liberation" with his intended "peace crusade." The essence of his aim was the same as that of Prime Minister Winston Churchill: "We arm to parley."

But with a difference. Whereas Churchill seemed ready to negotiate peace on the basis of the status quo, Dulles and Eisenhower were not. They aimed at compelling Communism to end the Cold War (a phrase coined by Herbert Bayard Swope in

1946) by negotiations. As Dulles explained (August 27, 1952), his plan for liberating the captive peoples did not include fomenting violent revolution. Instead, it counted on such "quiet" methods as "passive resistance, non-cooperation, encouraging discontent, slow-down and industrial sabotage." It would nourish resistance movements by "integrated air drops" and maintain communications with them through private organizations like the Committee for a Free Europe. Eventually the Communists' conquests "would disintegrate from within" and the "Russians would have to give up and go home."

This sort of talk pleased the people no end. The Republicans had railed at Truman's "immoral policy," not because it had gone wrong but because it had not gone far enough. They wanted to widen Acheson's "areas of strength" and, thanks to the extension, recover what had been lost to Communism by F.D.R. and Truman. Notably, in line with the views of MacArthur, they placed a much higher value than the Democrats on the Far East. And the Republican view was strong in both the Pentagon and the Congress.

But while unwilling to choose between vital areas, Eisenhower and Dulles accepted the priority of Europe. They too concentrated on the Truman-Acheson plan of encouraging the speedy formation of a European Defense Community that would include West Germany. Both Administrations believed this inclusion necessary if Europe was to resist Soviet pressures. Both Presidents also wanted a Middle East Common Plan of the kind the British had vainly been seeking.

Eisenhower and Dulles also intended to follow the Truman line of supporting the Organization of American States—only "better." They were ready to defy extreme anti-Communist Republicans by continuing American economic support to Tito of Yugoslavia. Dulles hoped for more Titos.

Admittedly, the new Administration had inherited an unstable, even sticky situation.

Continental Europe, thanks to Marshall Plan aid, was far enough on the road to economic recovery to resent dependence on America. France and Britain, in particular, had long and glorious traditions of independence and influence they found hard to forget. Moreover, British and French leaders who had greatly liked Acheson were suspicious of Dulles as a legal trickster.

In the Middle East, Egypt was feeling its oats and encouraging the other Arabs not to divert any of their growing truculence toward Israel against the U.S.S.R. or Communist imperialism. The weeping Mohammed Mossadegh of Iran, having confiscated the great British oil holdings, was plotting with the local Tudeh Party and with Moscow to oust the West completely.

In Latin America, resentment against the United States, strongest in Perón's Argentina, was rife. In large part this was jealousy of the greater North American largesse to Europe and parts of Asia than to the fellow American countries.[1]

And of course, the Korean war still dragged on, along with the endless negotiations with insolent Red Chinese at Panmunjom, while native revolt bogged down the French in Indo-China and the British in Malaya.

To complicate matters further, the new Administration had, by January, 1953, the certainty that the Soviet Union already possessed a stock of A-bombs sufficient to give thought to American strategic planners, who, since 1945, had been able to reckon on a monopoly of super-weapons, with all the theoretical freedom of action that went with such power.

Any way one looked at it, the Republicans' diplomatic task was enormous, and on this account, one may feel sure, even more attractive to the new Secretary of State. All his life John Foster

[1] In the budget year 1952-53, out of a six-billion-dollar mutual security appropriation, Latin America received less than seventy millions.

Dulles had trained for this great job. Now, thanks to the President's unlimited confidence in his judgment, Dulles had as free a hand as Congress would grant. Grasping the departmental reins firmly, he drove the policy chariot personally for six long years, traveling hundreds and hundreds of thousands of miles in the process.

Naturally he ran into a number of difficulties, some of them rooted in his own character, others in basic American attitudes.

The personal handicaps were chiefly two: first, in a world of anarchic power, Dulles was incurably legalistic; and second, to problems of clashing national interests he brought unswerving moral convictions that struck others as bigotry.

The Secretary of State was a "realist" about international law. To him it was not an amorphous web of precedents, customs and unenforceable promises, but a concrete fact that needed only to be recognized. Among innumerable examples of this attitude, I cite a convincing one from his own words. In *War or Peace* (1950) he wrote:

"I have never seen any proposal made for collective security with 'teeth' in it, or for 'world government' or for 'world Federation' which could not be carried out by the United Nations. . . ."

This was equivalent to stating that an international vigilance committee acting voluntarily was the same as a true executive enforcing the laws of a legitimate government. It led him to consider the United States as morally and legally bound by a commitment to the U.N. Charter which other countries flouted at will. Dulles required a "judicial and psychological foundation for intervention," thereby condemning his country to inaction in cases of indirect aggression.

His second handicap was not merely the conviction (shared by others) that "the greatest single political issue was the colonial issue"; no, Dulles felt that immediate national independence was a moral imperative which took precedence over the inhabitants' individual freedom and any political interest of the colonizing country. He acted accordingly—unlike Lincoln who put preservation of the Union above the right of "sovereign" American states to secede—and thereby weakened the West both militarily and economically. Neither the U.S.S.R. nor Red China (which preferred "power" to being "right") ever relinquished hold upon their "colonial" peoples nor did they appear to suffer exorbitantly "in the eyes of the world" for their failure to do so.

Purely American was the phenomenon known as McCarthyism, which divided and misled the nation and partially estranged Americans from the rest of the democratic world. Obviously, there existed a real need for eliminating from places of influence persons either favorable to Communism (or to the Soviet Union or to Red China) or obtuse to its danger. Adolf Berle, Jr., admitted that such a "real though feeble conspiracy" had developed during the honeymoon with Russia.[2]

Therefore, Senator McCarthy's charges of Communists in government (which he personally failed to prove) swept him to the top of a wave of popularity which the President lacked the means or the will successfully to counter. New and ill-drafted security regulations first formulated under Truman drove out of the government (and other jobs as well) not only a few Communists, pro-Communists and ex-Communists but others who, although they had served their country well, were considered for one reason or another as "security risks." McCarthy transformed his Senate Subcommittee into a Star Chamber which virtually tried suspected persons, in public and without proper legal safeguards, thus bringing American justice into international disrepute. His influence put a special security officer into the State Department whose demoralizing purges, unhappily, met little resistance from the great lawyer, John Foster Dulles.

Eventually, of course, McCarthy got his comeuppance. Con-

[2] Arthur Schlesinger, Jr., called the same conspiracy "pallid but vicious."

ceivably, he meant well but his unscrupulous methods were incompatible with American convictions more important than the elimination of a few subverted or questionable characters.

In the process of ousting "security risks," McCarthy divided the American people, partly along party lines, at a time when they needed unity. He offended allies who already disapproved of the United States and were only too ready to relax their anti-Communist efforts. And he misled many honest American citizens into believing that the "real" danger was not the powerful monolithic bloc of Communist states led by the U.S.S.R. but a few thousand Communists, sympathizers and dupes within the United States. This illusion made them all too ready to accept the new Administration's policy of defense economy at home.

Quite literally, the new "business" Administration set out to do *more* against Communism with *less*. The President and his first Cabinet (derided by Democrats as "eight millionaires and a plumber") were pledged to cut government expenditure—and did. There was room for economy. Government departments, including Defense, were cluttered with supernumerary employees and government spending everywhere was on the same high level as that of the rest of the "affluent society."

But to have eliminated excess employees and suppressed inequitable economic practices would have multiplied political opponents. So the President made the biggest cut in the one item where expansion rather than shrinkage was needed if the "bold new program" was to succeed—*defense spending*. The slogans became getting "a bigger bang for a buck," and obtaining "the greatest possible deterrent at bearable cost." Thanks to nuclear weapons, the first was temporarily possible. But the President, whose glorious military career led him to consider himself the foremost American expert on defense, went far beyond a shift from conventional to nuclear weapons. He and his economizing aides, two industrial magnates, Charles E. Wilson and George

Humphrey, respectively the lords of the Departments of Defense and of the Treasury, along with the Director of the Bureau of the Budget, decided that the Korean War expenditure, currently causing a deficit of ten billion dollars, was "endangering" the economy.

Almost their first act was to cut the missing ten billion from Truman's last budget, five billion of it from the Air Force alone. To justify this, they set forth the quaint theory that the Communist leaders were endeavoring to force the United States to "spend itself into bankruptcy" in an armament race. The Administration argued in defiance, or ignorance, of the Marxist dogma that spending on armaments is the recognized capitalist remedy for "overproduction."

Eisenhower, Wilson and Humphrey measured the defense by what they called the "long pull," a sort of "middle road between the security of a great mobilization achieved at crushing cost and a dangerous insecurity through failure to spend enough." All that was needed, they reckoned, was a "massive capacity to strike back." Not "force in being" but gross national product was "the basic element of national power," a theory which the U.S.S.R.'s possession of nuclear weapons had rendered obsolete. Nonetheless, with only minor modifications, the "long pull" defense policy lasted for eight long years. Wilson, in two drastic cuts, reduced the all-important appropriation for research and development of new weapons from sixteen billion to less than one billion dollars. As a result, America's preponderance of power shrank with each passing month.

Then in March, 1953, Stalin died. Some said his death was "assisted" by his trusted "enforcer," Lavrenty Beria who, with many others, was weary of Stalin's "cult of personality." Beria was soon to find that his associates were equally tired of him. Yet at the funeral, Stalin's immediate successor, Premier Georgi M. Malenkov, proclaimed his "new policy"—nothing less than "peaceful coexistence and competition between socialism and capitalism." (The phrase had been Stalin's, who said in 1927, "The basis of our relations with capitalist countries lies in the acceptance of the coexistence of two opposite systems.") Some maintained that Stalin himself had, just before he died, decided on this new zag in the U.S.S.R.'s tortuous course.

Malenkov's purpose was transparently to disarm Russia's chief adversaries by mollifying them while shifting the main Communist offensive from rapidly consolidating Europe back to Lenin's favorite targets, the weak nations and colonies of Asia, Africa and Latin-America. The new Soviet policy of "thaw" was, in short, a sort of political jujitsu designed to throw the adversary off balance in order to wound him mortally at his weakest spot.

Thus the new Premier led off with this: "There is not one disputed or undecided question that cannot be decided by peaceful means on the basis of mutual understanding of interested countries."

To emphasize the change, Malenkov partially relaxed police control at home and slightly shifted the economic program from heavy to consumer goods. On the other hand, he encouraged Red China to step up both military and political warfare in the Far East and rushed to completion Russia's first nuclear experiment.

Transparent the trick may have been, but it worked. Eisenhower quickly expressed the hope (April 16, 1953) that the "new leadership in Russia might do something for peace such as accepting an armistice in Korea and ending the indirect attacks upon Indo-China and Malaya." And though "not surprised" by the first Soviet nuclear explosion (August 12), he refused to allow any such episode to deflect him from reducing the American armed forces.[3] Instead, in deference to the "catastrophe of mod-

[3] David J. Dallin, *Soviet Foreign Policy After Stalin,* explains that to Molotov, a "lessening of tensions" meant recognition of Communism's conquests, abandonment of any attempt at liberation, abolition of overseas bases, and withdrawal from Europe by the United States.

ern war," he prepared what became his "atoms for peace plan." The Soviet "thaw" also drew applause from other Western countries eager for any pretext for avoiding domestic effort and allowing the West Germans to rearm.

Meanwhile, Winston Churchill, tipped off that Malenkov might be ready to pay a price to keep Germany disarmed, proposed nothing less than a new meeting of heads of state (of the sort that had proven so disastrous to the West at Teheran, Yalta and Potsdam during World War Two) that he thought would lead to "disengagement" and a "European settlement." [4]

All this was just what Russia sought. In fact Malenkov boasted publicly: "The North Atlantic bloc is now torn asunder by internal struggle and contradictions. If the tension is relaxed, the bloc may end in complete disruption."

The Soviet thaw also ended any chance the United States might have had of compelling Tito to relax his harsh grip on his own people and of spreading Titoism to other countries. For Titoism had been a result of Stalin's policy of building Communism in the U.S.S.R. at the expense of the other Communist countries. Once Malenkov (to be followed by Khrushchev) reverted to Communist internationalism, he removed the most plausible motive for further Communist secession. Nonetheless, Eisenhower and Dulles continued to hope for the further spread of Titoism.

Such were the circumstances and handicaps, in the face of which the new American Administration set out to liberate the victims of Communism by all pressures short of war (or infringement of international law).

Its first success was encouraging, cleverly ending the fighting in

[4] Thus, as the astute Philip Mosely quickly noted, "by showing slightly better manners in diplomacy, yet without conceding a single point of strength . . . Malenkov . . . allayed the . . . fears of many nations . . . and thus facilitated a substantial cutting back and postponement of rearmament plans in the free world." *The Kremlin and World Politics,* Vintage Books, 1960.

Korea. The President first ostentatiously sent atomic weapons to the front there. Then, in May, 1953, Dulles informed the "non-aligned" Nehru of India that the United States had decided to use these weapons against Chinese Manchuria if the war continued. (The President, however, explained that they could be used "only as a last resort.") Then Assistant Secretary of State Walter Robertson half-bullied, half-cajoled President Rhee of South Korea into accepting an armistice that would leave his country divided. Nobody could prevent Rhee, however, from liberating all those Chinese prisoners who did not wish to return to the Chinese People's Republic, an act which many Americans applauded.

Meanwhile, the President ordered the Seventh Fleet no longer to "shield Communist China." (Foreign Minister Eden of Britain and Prime Minister Nehru of India protested against this, but for once to no avail.)

And in consequence, on July 26, Red China's representatives at Panmunjom signed an armistice, although on terms strangely similar to those Truman had felt the American people would not accept. Some American Democrats insisted that the United Nations had accomplished its purpose, but most Americans had their doubts. The President consoled himself with the thought that Red Russia and Red China were not "natural allies," thus hinting at a future rupture. This line he probably got from Britons who were bent on pleasing Nehru, keeping Hong Kong and increasing their China trade. Actually, Britain simultaneously favored an Asian defense alliance, but one that omitted Japan, South Korea and Nationalist China.

Having thus ended the fighting in Korea, and warned Red China against new aggression of that type, Dulles turned his attention to helping France suppress the Communist-led rebellion in Indo-China. By the spring of 1954, the United States was paying seventy per cent of the cost of that war—which the French were not trying too hard to win.

The next victory came in August, 1953. Then, thanks to the brilliant diplomacy of the American Ambassador in Teheran, Loy Henderson, anti-Communist Iranian officers eliminated from power the pro-Communist Mossadegh. Soon thereafter, the foreign oil companies negotiated a new and generous oil contract with the Shah. The way was open for Iran to join its neighbors in a common front against Communism.

Then, patient American diplomacy finally settled the Yugoslav-Italian dispute over Trieste and western Istria.

Emboldened by these successes, Dulles (January 12, 1954) predicted boldly that if the United States maintained "a capacity for massive retaliation" in ways and at places of its own choosing, the Communist empire would "collapse from its own inner contradictions and distortions."

Admiral Arthur W. Radford, Chairman of the Joint Chiefs of Staff, had long felt that the United States must not spread its forces too thinly but rely for power upon a single strategic reserve. But Dulles' remark, caught and distorted by domestic opponents, convinced many jittery Europeans and Asians that Dulles was a political gambler. In fact, many considered the idea of a roll-back dangerous folly. Among these, surprisingly enough, was the aging Winston Churchill. He argued that, while a united world was better than a divided world, the latter was preferable to a world at war. "Provocation" was risky.

Undeterred by allied criticism or pressures for an accommodation with the "new" Soviet Union, Dulles moved forward as rapidly as the situation seemed to permit—and suffered two major defeats in the same year, through no fault of his own.

His first defeat was the French Parliament's repudiation of the European Defense Community Treaty, which the French Premier had accepted in 1952. For this defeat Americans, and notably Truman, were indirectly responsible. West Europe's security, including Britain's, depended upon America. Obviously, when

NATO was created in 1949-50, the United States could have insisted that not only West Germany but also British armies be integrated into the Community's single armed force, without distinction of nationality. Instead, Truman acquiesced in a British demand to stay out.

But Britain's abstention changed the whole picture for France. Without British participation, such a community could, Frenchmen feared, be dominated by Germany. Late in 1953, Dulles, realizing the growing danger of non-ratification by the French Parliament, warned Paris that repudiation could lead to an "agonizing reappraisal" of American policy toward Europe. Unimpressed, French nationalists and Communists combined to defeat ratification. The latter, richly supplied with funds by Moscow, waged a gigantic propaganda campaign, naturally on nationalistic rather than pro-Russian lines. The French Parliament finally voted down the Community, while fatuous French nationalists sang the *Marseillaise* to celebrate what was called the "turning point of post-war history and a major Soviet victory," by Suzanne Labin in her book, *Il Est Moins Cinq*.

American disappointment was great, not unmixed with indignation that after so much American help, Britain and France should sabotage a French proposal that offered, in American eyes, the best and cheapest method of defending all Europe.

Foreign Minister Anthony Eden soon realized, however, that too much opposition to the United States might bring about the "agonizing reappraisal" of American policy threatened by Dulles, and leave Europe, including Britain, in the lurch. He hastily offered to revive the moribund five-power Western Union (Brussels) Treaty (which had been concluded as a safeguard against a new *German* threat) to include West Germany. Thus the NATO force, including West Germany, came into being, though not as a single, integrated unit. Dulles then strengthened the alliance by a bilateral military agreement giving the United States bases in Franco's Spain.

Disappointed though he was, Dulles did not "reappraise" American policy, even though he had meanwhile been disappointed again by the same Franco-British combination in the Far East. The Republican Administration believed that America's Far Eastern troubles began when it failed to intervene to save Nationalist China. But Eisenhower and Dulles were reluctant to admit that, by accepting an armistice that left Korea divided, they had kicked the props out from under the French in Indo-China. For the Indo-China war was as unpopular in France as the Korean War had been in the United States.

Washington felt that Indo-China must be saved. Eisenhower explained to the American press that the countries of Southeast Asia were like a row of standing "dominoes" and that the fall of the first would bring about the fall of all, right down to Singapore and the borders of India. The armistice in Korea cleared the way for the Red Chinese to give massive aid to the rebels in Indo-China, the first "domino." Once Red China started supporting Communist Ho Chi-minh, the obvious way to thwart Ho was to defeat Red China. This was just what the American Administration had not done to save Korea. It chose something far less ambitious—the same threat of using nuclear weapons that had brought the Korean armistice.

The French Government wanted direct American military intervention. French Ambassador René Massigli in London said to Eden, "A single U.S. plane in the Indo-China sky and the situation is reversed." American military planners were not so sure. General Matthew Ridgway, Army Chief of Staff, felt that one and a half American infantry divisions would be required. Furthermore, the general feared that a defeat of Red China by the United States would be a victory for Soviet Russia since it would permit that latter to "move into the power vacuum thus created."

Other important Americans were, however, in favor of intervening. Dulles told France's Foreign Minister Bidault that we would "not accept the least progress of Communism in Southeast Asia. That's all over." A month later Dulles insisted that collective defense of the area was possible, regardless of the fate of beleaguered Dienbienphu. Vice President Nixon also favored intervention. But Congress, facing an election in the autumn, opposed American participation in any sort of war. And on the very day Dulles was talking collective defense to Bidault (April 24, 1954), the President, in Kentucky, was telling France's Ambassador Bonnet that intervention would "make the United States look like an imperialist." (The President had remarked in February that it "would be a tragedy to get into a hot war in Indo-China.")

As a result of this division, the Administration finally decided to intervene only if Britain and some other countries would participate, and meanwhile would persuade the French to promise immediate independence to the peoples of Indo-China. However, Prime Minister Churchill flatly refused to intervene. And the French showed little interest in carrying on a war for a territory which they had agreed to abandon.

After all the big talk, the President decided against further brinkmanship. For the third time in ten years, fear of Soviet power prevented the United States from eliminating the Chinese Communists. The United States did not intervene. Dienbienphu fell.

Premier Mendès-France, fearing that the war's unpopularity in France would strengthen Communism at home, agreed to negotiate, at Geneva, the division of Indo-China, with the Red Chinese, Britain and the U.S.S.R. as "mediators." After a brief appearance at the conference, the disgusted Dulles boycotted the proceedings, refusing to sign the offending treaty, and only grudgingly accepted its outcome which was a divided Vietnam, with Laos and Cambodia nominally independent, and represented another victory for Communism. Thereupon, encouraged by Ho Chi-minh's success in Indo-China, a group of Moslems almost immediately launched a revolt against France in Algeria—another toppling domino.

Dulles reacted as best he might to the loss of North Indo-China by creating the Southeast Asia Collective Defense Treaty, including the Philippines, Thailand, Pakistan, Australia, New Zealand, Britain and France. He later completed the ring by negotiating separate treaties with Japan, Nationalist China and South Korea. He promised Chiang Kai-shek not to reduce the size of the American garrison on Okinawa in exchange for Chiang's promise not to invade the Chinese mainland without consulting Washington. These alliances paid off when, at the Bandung Conference of 1955, many Asian nations publicly expressed their fear of Red China's new "super barbarism and super imperialism."

The Secretary of State compensated for the loss of strength in Britain's withdrawal from Suez, which he approved, and Egypt's refusal to cooperate with the West in defending the area, by creating and supporting (though not joining) the Baghdad Pact along the U.S.S.R.'s southern border.

That same year (1955) he really went to the "brink of war" with Red China in a successful effort to defend Formosa against Communists, while much of Europe shook in its shoes.

He steadily supported continental Europe's every effort toward economic or political unity against strong British opposition. Like Acheson before him, Dulles firmly believed that the inclusion of West Germany on an ultimately equal footing was essential to West Europe's defense, and to America's as well. Nor did he waver from his view that disunity alone was preventing West Europe from being a great, perhaps the greatest, center of spiritual, intellectual, economic and military force. Nor would he countenance the notion of some Britons that their role was to "reconcile the two giants before war came." They believed that sweet talk, the multiplication of non-aligned and buffer states and other concessions to the U.S.S.R.'s "legitimate fears" would "accelerate the evolution in Russia and end the Cold War." Dulles disagreed.

Dulles, in fact, had little use for neutral states unless, like Tito's Yugoslavia, they were recruited from the orthodox Communist camp. He believed that, to survive, the free world must win the Cold War and he considered that any country wishing to remain free had an ethical duty to join Moscow's opponents. This brought him into a direct clash with Prime Minister Jawaharlal Nehru of India, who, seeing little difference between Moscow Communists and Western "imperialists," thought to serve peace by converting as many free nations as possible from the anti-Communist to the "nonaligned" camp, while ultimately relying upon the United States for protection from Communism.[5]

When India invited the Russian leaders for a visit, Dulles publicly condemned neutralism as immoral and shortsighted. Many throughout the world disagreed violently, among them British and French leaders. Statesmen in both London and Paris had drunk heavily of Malenkov's proffered cup of "peaceful coexistence." As early as the Bermuda conference of 1953 both Prime Minister Churchill and Premier Laniel of France recommended a Summit Meeting with Malenkov. Dulles saw no good in any such meeting until, under Western pressure, the Soviets revised their policy. To him, the Summit offer was just another example of clever Soviet propaganda. In *War or Peace,* he had written:

"Soviet communism has the advantage of the offensive. It has no counteroffensive to fear, either in propaganda or the Cold War. It can push its redivision of the world, picking the time and place for its offensive and knowing that it can consolidate its gains at leisure."

[5] In 1951, even before Dulles became Secretary of State, Nehru went into a tantrum when I mentioned his name in the course of a discussion of Korea.

Nothing had happened to make him change his views, but the British and French persisted. Heartened by their success in ending the war in Indo-China and by Dulles' failure to carry out his "agonizing reappraisal" of American foreign policy, they demanded that a "real effort" be made to smoke out Soviet intentions. At the United Nations late in 1954, Mendès-France publicly insisted that France was "ready to meet the Russians at the highest level."

Soviet strategy was as plain as the bulbous dome of Saint Basil's Church on the Red Square in Moscow. Yet Eisenhower, despite, or perhaps because of, his military career, had become less interested in any speedy liberation of the captive peoples than in becoming a great peacemaker. Since Churchill and others believed the Russians might be ready for peace, then surely there could be no harm in finding out. To be sure, the President hedged a little. He stated publicly that the United States would go "to any length consistent with our concepts of *decency* and *justice* to obtain peace." (My italics.) So, of course, would Dulles, but he felt that leaving the captive peoples under the Bear's paw was inconsistent with decency and justice.

Yet arguments other than Churchill's were driving Eisenhower toward the Summit. Tenaciously as he held to the "finite deterrent" and limited spending for defense, he was too much a general not to realize the new danger latent in Soviet possession of nuclear weapons. In fact, he had said in October, 1954, that "since the advent of nuclear weapons there is no longer any alternative to peace."[6] By January, 1955, his military planning no longer assumed any spectacular American military advantage over the U.S.S.R. Yet the successful Soviet arms drive was rendering Amer-

[6] This seemed very like an echo of the cunning admission of Malenkov (March, 1954) that "with the existence of modern weapons of destruction [war] would mean the destruction of world civilization."

ica's limited arms policy dangerous. Among other economies, it had entailed a cut in research on guided missiles. Yet the Administration had known for many years of the frantic Soviet effort to produce both long- and short-range rockets.[7] The President's alternatives were either an end to the arms race by controlled disarmament or more spending or eventual Soviet superiority.[8]

Since 1946, the United States had favored the abolition of atomic (later nuclear) weapons under proper control. Ever since, desultory disarmament talks in the framework of the United Nations had dragged on with no apparent progress. Since the NATO countries relied chiefly on the atomic deterrent in the hands of the United States, they could only give it up as a part of complete disarmament. Yet pacifist and liberal elements everywhere unceasingly demanded an end to the "stalemate of terror."

The decisive argument in favor of the Summit was the President's desire to see a Conservative Party victory in the British general election of 1955. Some Labor Opposition leaders were both appeasement-minded and anti-American.[9] Even Dulles recognized the mounting pressure. The best he could do was obtain a price for American consent to a Summit Meeting with the Russians. This was a peace treaty freeing little Austria from over ten years of military occupation, but neutralizing that country. This concession, which cut direct military communications between West Germany and Italy, was no surrender by Russia. But at the treaty ceremony in the Belvedere Palace in Vienna, Dulles amazed his colleagues and delighted optimistic Europeans pres-

[7] Admiral William Parsons told me in the late Forties of the rising Soviet missile threat and also that the U.S. Air Force saw little need for our meeting it at the time.

[8] The Killian Report to the President in the winter of 1954-55 recommended a speedup of the production of ICBM's, and parallel development of ICBM's both by the Army and to be launched from ships. The President waited several months before accepting the program.

[9] The late Aneurin Bevan told me that if he were Chinese, he would "be a Communist."

ent by publicly hugging Molotov, whom he generally considered his chief opponent. British Conservatives won the election. The way was clear for the first Summit Meeting since Truman went to Potsdam in 1945.[10]

Several major topics confronted the heads of the four states who met at Geneva in the sunny July weather of 1955 and in the brightest glare of publicity since the Peace Conference at Paris in 1919. These were disarmament, the reunification of Germany and a European security system.

Actually the three Western delegations were divided on policy and no amount of preliminary consultation could have united them. The British and the French leaders passionately wanted disarmament but were, to say the least, cool on seeing a united Germany. (Chancellor Adenauer, who was summering in the nearby Swiss Alps, expected neither unification nor disarmament, but could not say so.[11])

Eisenhower arrived full of enthusiasm. He somehow counted on growing Soviet military strength to make the Russians pliant, both on the reduction of armaments and the unification of Germany, since they had nothing to fear. On the eve of his departure from the United States, he had stated that the American people wanted to be friends with the Russian people. Since the Russian people were in no sense present or represented, this statement seemed irrelevant. But the President's enthusiasm was contagious. Perhaps—who knew?—something good could come out of it. He literally opened his arms to the Soviets when he greeted his "old friend Marshal Zhukov."

Soviet President Bulganin and Premier Khrushchev, who had

[10] Even Dulles was finally convinced that the Soviet peace truce was a "sign of the growing instability of the Communist regime."

[11] When the French Parliament killed the European Defense Community, Adenauer warned Dulles to "make the best use of the time I am alive to cement West Germany to the Free World. When I am gone it will be too late."

ousted Malenkov, made the most of the occasion. Neglecting the British and French leaders, who had expected to play again the same dominating role they had at the Geneva conference on Indo-China, they made a dead set for the American President.

Presumably the conference might have "succeeded" if the United States had given the Russians what they wanted—a specific recognition of the existing situation in East Germany and East Europe. But neither the President nor his Secretary of State would go that far. Therefore they got no nearer to disarmament, a united Germany or a European security system. Instead, they scored a temporary propaganda success when Eisenhower, at the last moment, drew "out of his hat" a well-prepared offer of "open skies" inspection of possible preparations for attack, a brain child of Nelson Rockefeller. This offer pleased anxious souls everywhere and led the usually critical Paris newspaper *Le Monde* to call Eisenhower "the type of leader humanity needs today."

The Russians, on the other hand, got something beyond their wildest dreams—*the certainty that they could continue their expansion through propaganda, subversion and even military probing without fear of a sudden American attack.* For, on the second day of the conference, while the President was trying to convince the Russians that West Germany's participation in NATO was no threat to them, he suddenly turned in his chair and said:

"I would particularly like my friend, Marshal Zhukov, to listen carefully to what I now have to say.... He knows that, speaking as soldier to soldier, I have never uttered a single word that I did not believe to be true.... Personally, I have had enough of war and I would not have accepted that [NATO] command had I conceived it to be an organization getting ready to fight a war.... The United States is a fairly important member of NATO, and I can assure you that *under no circumstances is the United States ever going to be a party to aggressive war—against any nation.*"[12]

The President's remark was an all but inconceivable political concession. To most Americans it seemed banal enough. But to the Russians it was the door opened to unlimited expansion provided only that they refrained from a direct attack on some part of the world that interested the United States. No longer any fear that a carefully provoked military uprising in say, Cuba or the Congo, wherein the hand of Moscow was conspicuous, would trigger an American attack upon the U.S.S.R. or Red China. The chief obstacle to an all-Red world was removed by the man Moscow regarded as its chief opponent. Unhappily the President's moral appeal meant nothing to fanatics steeped in the certainty of the inevitable triumph of Communism—and their duty to hasten it.

Meanwhile, unmindful of the President's fateful boner, "all the world," as Richard Rovere noted, seemed to "think that the conference itself was wonderful." In so judging, the world exhibited an unequaled incomprehension.

As at all unsuccessful modern conferences, the governments sought to hide their failure behind a subsequent foreign ministers' conference in the autumn. The failure of the second conference destroyed the so-called "spirit of Geneva." Although expected by experienced persons, the double fiasco proved a bitter blow to many, for example, the editor of a certain liberal American weekly. He had commissioned an article on the Geneva Summit and refused to publish it when the author explained why the conference left the free world worse off than before. Why should he, when the President announced that "the prospects of a lasting peace with justice, well-being and broader freedom" were "greater"?

Yet the fiasco of the second Geneva conference was the turning

[12] Quoted in *America and the World of Our Time,* by Jules Davids. The italics are mine.

point for the Eisenhower Administration. It marked the end of "roll-back." The "bold new program" collapsed. Thereafter, the Administration sought peace rather than liberation and the "relaxation of tensions" rather than the "prosecution of the Cold War . . . with vigor and wisdom" promised by the President.

Chapter VIII

EISENHOWER BUYS TIME

"Optimism is a mania for declaring that all is well when things are going badly."

—VOLTAIRE

From the Summit Meeting of 1955 until 1961 the West's fortunes moved, with sporadic pick-ups, steadily down.

Shortly after this meeting, at which he gave away his ace-in-the-hole (the Soviet belief that he might launch a sudden destructive attack against a persistently aggressive U.S.S.R. or Red China), the President was away from his desk for seven weeks with a severe heart attack. What went on in his mind as he lay in Colorado under threat of death he has not told. Judged by his subsequent conduct, one may imagine that he then decided that if he recovered sufficiently to run again and retain the Presidency, he would devote his second term overwhelmingly to the cause of peace.

It was a noble ambition. Unhappily, it overlooked Mr. Dooley's ancient dictum that the one thing a free man or country cannot refuse to give another man or country, if it insists, is a fight. And at no time since 1917 had the Kremlin given any convincing sign of wanting peace on any but its own terms. Still less had it renounced its worldwide imperialism. Those who were waiting for the change might wait a long time—and lose both freedom and peace in the process. President Syngman Rhee was arguing that nobody could, without loss, coexist with Communists. The President's refusal to acknowledge this transformed his quest for "peace with honor and justice" into moonshine. But Dwight D. Eisenhower knew, or at least hoped for, better. Therefore, to the end of his Administration he continued to seek the friendship of Soviet leaders who talked peaceful coexistence and waged Cold War.

The Utopian character of any such quest had become indelibly clear at that abortive Summit Meeting. Without exactly saying so, Western leaders accepted the division of Europe, which was tacit recognition of Stalin's wartime conquests. After 1955, with a few brief interludes, Dulles directed his "inflexibility" primarily against his allies. "Massive retaliation," "liberation," "agonizing reappraisal"? Gone with the nuclear monopoly!

The change in policy became visible in the Middle East during the Presidential campaign of 1956. Since 1948, the history of this area had been one of clashing elements: the new State of Israel carved from once Arab (Turkish) Palestine; Europe's dependence upon and American investments in Mideastern oil; rising Arab nationalism directed not only against Israel but against the "exploiters" of both the oil wells and the Europe-planned-and-built Suez Canal; Dulles' curious assumption that nationalist Arabs would welcome American influence as a substitute for the hated British and French presence; and, finally, to come back to it again, the "hunting license" given Bulganin and Khrushchev by Eisenhower at the Geneva Summit.

Establishing a Jewish homeland in Palestine might have been a mistake in 1917 (when Wilson backed it wholeheartedly) but after Hitler's slaughter of Jews, not all of Ernest Bevin's pro-Arab shenanigans could prevent it. The Arabs lost their best chance to do so when unorganized Israel defeated three of their five invading armies and stalemated the other two.

This defeat at the hands of barely armed Israelis brought Arab nationalism to a slow boil. Shortly thereafter, King Farouk of Egypt denounced the Suez treaty with Britain and summoned Britain to remove its troops from the Canal zone. Next, nationalistic Egyptian officers ousted Farouk, fomented riots against British garrisons and insisted the British get out. Dulles morally supported this demand. In July, 1954, the British promised the Egyptian dictator, Gamal Abdel Nasser, to withdraw their forces from Egypt within twenty months. They still hoped he would cooperate in a joint area security system. When he refused, Dulles created without joining, and Britain joined, the Baghdad alliance along the southern border of Russia, with one Arab member, Iraq. The obdurate Nasser then demanded, and got, a promise of economic assistance from Britain and the United States.

As a good Levantine, Nasser knew the advantages of working both sides of an international street. Communist Tito of Yugoslavia, twice saved from ruin by the United States but stubbornly "neutral," gave him excellent advice on how to make the most of non-alignment. The U.S.S.R. was only too happy to get into the once forbidden Middle Eastern pasture. In exchange for unsaleable cotton, it supplied Egypt with modern arms. Thus encouraged, the Arab states stepped up their guerrilla raids into Israel—a favorite Arab pastime since their defeat in 1948. In April, 1956, Egypt, Syria, Saudi Arabia and Yemen publicly announced the formation of a united command against Israel. In June the last British forces left Egyptian soil.

But Nasser overreached himself. Britain had warned the world that it would, if necessary, fight in defense of its Mideast oil supplies. France was fed up with Nasser's open (and illegal) support of the Algerian rebels. Paris supplied Israel with first-class planes and field equipment.

Meanwhile, the United States, annoyed by Nasser's deals with Communism and recognition of Red China, first delayed and then canceled a previous offer of funds to help Egypt build a great dam at Aswan on the Nile. A few days later, Nasser announced the nationalization of the Suez Canal Company. Future tolls from the canal would, he said, be used for financing the dam.

Britain froze Egyptian funds in British banks, promptly dispatched warships to the area and hinted at military mobilization. France made a common front with Britain. Dulles hurried home from a Peruvian visit and started working for a negotiated solution that would satisfy Britain and France without overly angering the Arabs. The task proved to be beyond him.

One reason was his inability to get along with Anthony Eden, now Prime Minister. Eden privately accused Dulles of tedious moralizing, of using imprecise language to hide disagreements, of being "over-friendly" to Chancellor Adenauer of West Germany and of being insensitive to Britain's vital interests. Dulles could not forget Britain's hasty recognition of Red China, its pressure for stopping the Korean fighting, its part in torpedoing the European Defense Community, its refusal to intervene in Indo-China and its insistence on a premature and futile Summit Meeting. He did not deny that the Anglo-American alliance was the keystone of the West but he certainly felt that too often the junior partner had had the last word. This time it was going to be different.

The American Secretary sought an "international system" that would operate the canal in the name of Egypt. But Nasser opposed any sort of international control. Britain and France would take nothing less. They stepped up military preparations, sending troopships and aircraft carriers to the Mediterranean. U.S. diplomats in London and Paris warned Dulles that this time London and Paris meant business.

By September, the crisis was acute, but the American people were too fascinated by the fun of electing a President to care.

Dulles, by indecision or design, blew alternately hot and cold. Meanwhile, Britain and France slowly built up enough force to seize the canal; the Arabs made ready to destroy Israel; and Israel, with France's connivance, planned to blitz Egypt!

On October 25, the Chief of Staff of Jordan announced that the time had come to eliminate the Jewish State. Instead, four days later, Israeli armies invaded Sinai and the Gaza Strip and, while the other Arab nations looked on, proceeded to smash the Communist-armed Egyptian forces. Within forty-eight hours, the Israelis had occupied most of the Sinai Peninsula and islands in the Gulf of Aqaba, which Egypt had been using for harassment, and had taken six thousand prisoners. Had the British and French immediately landed parachutists along the west side of the canal, at the same time rushing a heavy tank column overland to consolidate their position, they and the Israelis might have had the canal intact. Instead, after twenty-four hours, they sent a deliberately misleading ultimatum to Egypt and to Israel, ordering both to evacuate the canal zone. This gave Nasser time to block the canal with sunken ships. Both belligerents naturally ignored the ultimatum. (French fliers were protecting Israel.) After three days more, an incredibly sluggish Franco-British expeditionary force landed at Port Said, with all the precautions of a full-fledged military campaign against a major adversary.

Nasser was on the verge of flight. But twenty-four hours before the invaders could reach Cairo, the United States, joined by the U.S.S.R., the Communist satellites and the non-aligned Asian-African nations, called for a cease-fire and sternly requested the three "invaders" to withdraw.

Aided by Dulles, Eisenhower prepared and gave a television and radio speech which made no mention of Nasser's assault on really vital interests of our friends. Instead, the President stressed the need for a "single code of international conduct" and for law as the only basis for peace. (The U.S.S.R. suggested that, if necessary, Russia and America should "join forces" and stop the fighting!)

The British and French Governments received all this with consternation. Prime Minister Anthony Eden, voted down seventeen to one in his own Cabinet, resigned with broken health. Anti-American feeling rose high among the French and British while pacifists and liberals in the United States rejoiced. So did those other Americans who rated the good will of the undeveloped peoples above the military strength of major allies. Recriminations flew back and forth across the Atlantic. For the nasty fact was, as Jules Davids noted in *America and the World of Our Time*, "Freedom for colonial peoples inevitably weakened the power positions of the Western European countries and tended to create a political vacuum."

Nasser in fact showed his gratitude by practically inviting the Communist camp into that vacuum, thereafter calling for instant bloody insurrection throughout Africa and seeking to re-create the once mighty Arab empire under his personal rule. Although the Israelis withdrew from Sinai and the Gaza Strip only when promised free transit through the canal by the United Nations and the American President, Nasser insolently refused to comply. Nor did Eisenhower, chief author of the withdrawal, ever seriously seek to compel Egypt's compliance.[1]

All this was bad enough. But a worse crisis was simultaneously in progress in Eastern Europe. The Soviet thaw, particularly Khrushchev's public condemnation of Stalin's "excesses" and "cult of personality," had encouraged the captive populations of that

[1] Emboldened by the impunity of Nasser, Morocco a few years later repaid American support for its independence from France (1954) by summoning the Americans to withdraw gradually from the great air bases—bastion of free world power—built there with the consent of France and confirmed by the new state. In 1961, Egypt and Morocco took the lead in organizing the anti-West forces of Africa. To be sure, this was done under cover of "nonalignment" and with the prospect of continued baksheesh from both sides.

area to strive openly for "national Communism" and greater freedom.

Heartened by rioting in Poznań, Poland, in June, 1956, the Hungarians demanded the punishment of their Communist leaders, one of whom, Rakosi, was a sort of monster against whom Tito, momentarily reconciled with Khrushchev, had warned the latter. But instead of replacing him with the popular Nagy, Khrushchev installed a more stupid Rakosi, Gerö by name. On October 19, the threat of open revolt by the Polish Communist leaders, backed by a rashly courageous people hostile both to Communism and to Russian domination, compelled Khrushchev to accept a considerable loosening of the Communist vise. On October 23, Budapest rebelled. Thousands of students, police and soldiers rallied to the side of the rebels. (So, too, did some members of the Soviet garrison.) The revolt rapidly spread throughout the country. Soviet tank commanders were reluctant to repress it. Mikoyan and Suslov flew from Moscow to Budapest and, after consultations, substituted Nagy for Gerö. On October 28, all Soviet armed forces began to withdraw from Budapest, announcing that they were quitting Hungary.

But by this time the people were demanding more than a change of tyrant. Moscow dutifully announced a revision of the entire oppressive relationship with its East European "socialist" neighbors.

Dulles must have been jubilant. Here was the expected dissolution of the Soviet Empire. And, for the first time since World War Two, continental Europeans, including the French, were ready to cooperate with the United States in aiding the embattled Hungarian rebels. Why was Washington waiting to recognize Nagy? Where were the observers from the United Nations?

Yet even while Nagy was announcing Hungary's withdrawal from the Warsaw Pact and its new neutrality on the Yugoslav model, Soviet leaders, after a tense meeting in the Kremlin, decided to crush the revolt. On November 4, while both the United States and the United Nations were concentrating on the crisis at Suez, the Russians struck back at Nagy and his rebels by force and treachery.

Why the reversal? Chiefly, one must surmise, because Eisenhower, in a public speech, insisted that the United States *had no intention of interfering with the security of the Soviet Union.*

While the Soviets were refastening their claws in Hungarian flesh, the President was on the trans-Atlantic telephone lecturing Eden on the iniquity of British and French aggression against Egypt.

Once the Kremlin realized that Washington intended nothing more serious than a protest on Hungary, it impudently threatened to destroy Paris and Berlin with missiles.

The U.S.S.R. was the real beneficiary of both crises. The Suez affair allowed the Soviet to enter the power void in the Middle East left by the Franco-British retreat. *American inertia in Hungary marked the turning point in the Cold War.* While the Soviets, as always, preferred power to popularity, the Americans chose the fiction of international law. American prestige, essentially a function of power and the will to use it, began to sag into the slump from which it never recovered during the Presidency of Dwight D. Eisenhower.

What would have happened had the United States taken the exactly opposite course of keeping the Soviets out of Hungary while letting the Franco-British-Israeli combination oust Nasser and internationalize the Suez Canal? These steps together might have started an anti-Soviet chain reaction in Europe and stabilized the Near East for several years. Even more important, saving Hungary and eliminating Nasser would have united NATO as never before, and for years to come. To be sure, doing both simultaneously would have taken high brinkmanship by the man, Dulles, who was later criticized for having frequently gone to the edge of war. Yet the Soviet's hesitancy in reoccupying Hungary until sure of American inertia argues that the Kremlin would not have accepted major war to prevent the emergence of a second Tito in Hungary.[2]

Against such concrete advantages, the abstract disapproval of non-aligned Asian-Africans would have weighed little.

Instead, NATO was all but disrupted. Anglo-American relations went into a slump that ended only with Anthony Eden's resignation and a complete about-face by his successor, Harold Macmillan.

Eisenhower and Dulles received the extravagant plaudits of many sincere people who either put the avoidance of war risk above all else or who, like F.D.R. fifteen years earlier, managed to believe that, given enough American patience, the U.S.S.R. would see the error (or the danger) of its ways. Yet the American leaders must have had some inkling that in November, 1956, their anti-colonialism had outstripped their statesmanship. For shortly thereafter, a re-elected Eisenhower warned the Soviets against threatening the Baghdad Pact nations and (in the spring of 1957) persuaded the Congress to endorse an *Eisenhower Doctrine* which not only declared the independence and integrity of Middle Eastern nations vital to American security, but announced that America was prepared to use force to assist any nation or nations "requesting assistance against armed aggression from any country controlled by international communism." [3]

Despite the bold announcement, the United States steadily showed itself less disposed than the U.S.S.R. to risk a showdown, even when monopoly of the A-bomb precluded the possibility of

[2] So objective a historian as Seton-Watson argued that the United States could have saved Hungary (and perhaps later the rest of East Europe) without a war. Certainly, the Soviet threat to destroy London and Paris was sheer rodomontade.

[3] This said nothing that had not been in the Truman Doctrine of March, 1948.

an American defeat.[4] Moreover, *neither Truman nor Eisenhower was ready to create the kind of force necessary to win local wars anywhere on the globe.* Nor were the other NATO countries, and like the United States, they laid the blame on their alleged "inferiority in manpower" to the "Soviet hordes." This was at best a bad joke. For the NATO countries together had a greater able-bodied population than the U.S.S.R. and its European satellites. They were capable, if necessary, of matching the Communist forces division for division and then some, not to speak of maintaining a superiority in nuclear weapons. That they refused was a matter of choice, not of necessity. They would not divert the men and money from their main goal—a higher living standard.

In the United States, economy in defense not only brought about a reduction of conventional forces but also a lag in the production of missiles and space programs. President Eisenhower came to the White House mysteriously believing that a "sound economy" was the main source of national strength (something that it had ceased to be in the nuclear age when only weapons-in-being counted) and that the main source of a sound economy was a balanced budget. Once his two chief advisers, Secretary Humphrey at the Treasury and Secretary Wilson at Defense, persuaded him that forty billion dollars annually was about all that the American economy could stand without "dislocation," he stuck to this figure. The result, according to Roscoe Drummond and Gaston Coblentz in *Duel at the Brink,* was that "a cumulative shift of the balance of power against the United States became the dominant tragic fact of the Dulles era."

The explanation seemed to be that the President considered a nation's military strength not primarily as the indispensable support of its political policy in peace or war but merely as the safe-

[4] As a result, between April, 1950, and June, 1959, Red Russia and Red China made at least sixteen unprovoked attacks on American planes, any one of which would have provoked trouble in the pre-nuclear age.

guard of its security. His aim, therefore, became the maintenance of just enough power to prevent the Russians and other Communists from launching a successful blitz attack upon the United States. Anything more, he thought, was money wasted. Instead, he concentrated more and more on seeking disarmament. For he had come to believe that in the nuclear age there was "no alternative to peace"—or, at least, being left in peace.

What he sought was a modus vivendi, or way of living with imperialistic Communism, until such time as it lost its venom or succumbed to a superior economic system. Eventually, in this analysis, the Soviets would themselves limit Communism's expansion lest it put too great a strain upon their resources.

General Eisenhower believed that with modern weapons, "enough is certainly aplenty and you do no good, as I see it, by increasing those numbers, except to get, say, an added factor of safety." Anything like permanent preponderance would constitute an "overkill" or an indulgence in the "numbers racket." (May 10, 1956.)

Nor did his obsession with minimum defense stop here. He looked upon military preponderance as dangerous in itself. "Any nation," he once said, "that tried [to keep military strength equal to all its commitments] *would itself become a potential menace to the peace.* We should then have one power dominating the world by its ever apparent military might. The mere existence of such a power would be an invitation to all other peoples to combine against it." [5]

Such a notion, conceivably true in a multi-state system where

[5] Quoted by Merlo Pusey in *Eisenhower the President* (my italics). Eisenhower may have acquired this idea from his Secretary of Defense, who had stated that "too big a force on our part might convince most of the people on earth that we were going to start trouble." In any case, several years later, he found a disciple in Britain's Foreign Secretary, the Earl of Home, who stated in Paris (Dec. 23, 1960) that "the danger of war does not arise from the balance of power; that comes when one side or other achieves a decisive superiority in arms."

many states could collectively outarm any single state, simply ceased to be exact in a world divided into two hostile blocs, either of which, if permitted, could develop the strength sufficient to overcome the resistance of all other states and thereby conquer the planet—the avowed Communist aim.

In consequence, America's relative military potential fell steadily, both in conventional forces and in the production of jet aircraft and guided missiles.

Then, on October 4, 1957, the Soviet Union capped a prolonged and determined effort to overtake the United States' lead in nuclear weapons by successfully launching something it called the first "fellow traveler of the earth" (in Russian, "Iskusstvennyi Sputnik Zemly"). Therewith, the U.S.S.R. publicly challenged the United States' military preponderance. Human life moved into a new dimension.

Outclassed in the A-bomb and manned airplanes, Soviet rulers had turned in 1945 to developing the German wartime V-2 rocket into a weapon that, equipped with a nuclear warhead, could destroy any unprotected spot on the planet. The Sputnik of 1957 was propelled by a rocket with a thrust of about a million pounds, several times as powerful as any then developed by the United States. Thereafter, no spot in America was secure from obliteration.

How did the Administration react to this Soviet triumph of which it had been warned by monitors in Turkey? President Eisenhower told a news conference that it had "*no military significance*" and would make "*not one iota of difference to the security of the free world.*" (My italics.) "Engine Charley" Wilson called it a "nice Soviet trick" but no reason for speeding up defense at home since "it would be pretty unpopular to increase taxes to the point necessary." Another great brain in high office called the Soviet satellite a "silly bauble." Still another compared its launching to playing "space basketball."

On the other hand, Senator Richard B. Russell of Georgia, Chairman of the Senate Armed Services Committee, commented, to his honor, that the future of the United States might well be "at stake."

Shortly thereafter, America's foremost military authority administered yet another dose of verbal soothing syrup to a worried people. The gist of it was: we're doing fine, don't worry. So if, as one historian wrote, "the American people enjoying an unprecedented prosperity had neither the purpose nor the will to stay ahead in the missile and space races,"[6] the fault was not really theirs.

Nor was it the fault of American scientists. To be sure, from 1945 to 1950, the Truman Administration, lacking an atomic warhead sufficiently small to be carried by a rocket, and discouraged by the Air Force (which saw no reason to hasten its own decline), did practically nothing to develop the new weapon. But by 1950, the Army, thanks to its German rocketeers, had "the finest missile team in the world." Yet interservice rivalries and misplaced defense economy slowed down accomplishment.

After Sputnik One, General Curtis LeMay, chief of the Strategic Air Command upon which the safety of the West chiefly depended, warned that without greater American bomb yield, the U.S.S.R. would between 1958 and 1960 have greater striking power than the United States. And slowly the American leviathan jolted into action. But by then it would take some years to fill the missile gap. Yet still the complacent President shrank from ordering a crash program.[7]

He remained so calm that he ignored advisers who argued that, while seeking disarmament and relaxation of tensions, he might, at least, regain some diplomatic initiative and ease the stalemate

[6] John W. Spanier, *American Foreign Policy Since World War Two.*

[7] Two interesting accounts of this struggle are: *Polaris* by James Baar and William E. Howard, and *Reaching for the Stars* by Erik Bergaust.

of terror by embarking on a civilian shelter program. Never before in America's history had any President so often overridden his chiefs of staff or had so many top military leaders felt called upon to protest against this or that facet of a presidential defense policy.[8] The President even suppressed or cold-shouldered the recommendations of several ad hoc investigating commissions he himself set up.

Nevertheless, the great Soviet achievement did spark a space and missile race with the United States—winner take all. Eisenhower had first insisted that the United States was "rapidly filling the gap" (October 28, 1958), then that he was "amazed about this business of catching up" since "what you want is enough, a thing that is adequate" (February 11, 1960). But whatever the President wanted, the rest of the world, allies, neutrals and enemies alike, suspected that the United States was no longer a dependable protector, or the dominant power, or an adversary to be greatly feared.

The effect upon America's allies was profound. Before 1957 each Soviet advance or threat had heightened their interest in alliance; thereafter Soviet belligerence (and their own returning prosperity) resulted in a search for some alternative or supplement to the American link. For if they could not depend upon the certainty of American readiness to wage war in their defense, or on America's ability to deter a possible attack or to win a nuclear war, they had to look elsewhere.

The British government moved further toward onesided conciliation, advocating American recognition of Red China, popular-front governments and non-alignment for threatened countries, even a "new status" for West Berlin. Part of the British Opposition recommended an end to the American alliance and unilateral nuclear disarmament. In January, 1961, the leader of the Canadian

[8] The list included Admirals Radford and Rickover; Generals Ridgway, Taylor, Gavin, Medaris and Power, to mention only the most prominent.

Opposition urged his government to pull out of the North American Air Defense Command with the United States, lest Canada be compelled to house nuclear weapons on Canadian soil—and become a potential target.

President de Gaulle of France urged a reorganization of NATO with a three-power directorate to plan common strategy everywhere. Meanwhile, he hastened to produce those nuclear weapons which Congress stubbornly refused to share with its closest allies. Some French leftists combined with Communists to advocate appeasement of Russia.

Out of once granite-firm Turkey came voices suggesting possible non-alignment as a substitute for the American alliance. Even manly Pakistanis began to wonder whether their undeveloped country would not do better to pull out of the Central Treaty Organization and SEATO and accept help from both sides, as India was doing. In Japan, the trend toward breaking the American alliance, neutralism and closer relations with Red China grew steadily.

How could it have been otherwise after Secretary of State Herter, who succeeded Dulles, stated before the Senate Foreign Relations Committee before his appointment that he could see no possibility of America waging a nuclear war unless directly attacked?

Most of the newly liberated countries decided on non-alignment, convinced by the example of Yugoslavia and the United Arab Republic—both saved by America at different times—that they could receive generous American aid while opposing American policies and have American protection without cost or inconvenience. In fact, many liberated colonies quickly gravitated into pro-Communism.

More amazing, American authorities watched approvingly while a bearded Cuban revolutionary, allied with professional Communist agents, "liberated" his country from the evil dictator

Batista, and then, to the astonishment of these authorities, transformed it into the first Soviet bastion in the Western Hemisphere.

In once-allied Iraq, Brigadier General Abdul Karim Kassem, with Communist support, murdered the King and the pro-Western Prime Minister and set up an anti-Western regime. Yet the United States restrained a Turkish impulse to eject him.

To be sure, in the Mediterranean and in the Far East, the formidable U.S. Sixth and Seventh Fleets, respectively, were on guard. But their presence would have been more reassuring to threatened nations but for one fact: while Eisenhower refrained from expensive defense measures, such as those recommended in the Rockefeller and suppressed Gaither and Coolidge reports, lest they diminish the changes of a negotiated settlement, Khrushchev frantically concentrated on increasing his already formidable armory, boasted of a new "fantastic weapon" to come, and started civil defense drill for his most exposed human targets.

In fact, politically buttressed by the prestige of the Sputniks, Red Russia and Red China went to town. Twice, to be sure, they were turned back by the United States, once in conjunction with Great Britain. In the summer of 1958, American Marines in Lebanon and British paratroopers in Jordan prevented the absorption of these two countries by either pro-Communist Egypt or by fanatically anti-West Iraq. In the autumn, when Red China, with Soviet consent, again murderously shelled the Nationalist-held offshore islands, the United States quelled the outburst by stating clearly that it would, if necessary, fight to prevent their conquest. Whereupon Khrushchev persuaded Mao to call off the bombardment.

These were the last bold moves of the now mortally ailing Dulles. Red China surreptitiously seized a section of northern India and, in defiance of its solemn promise, goaded the patient Tibetans into a revolt, resulting in the flight of the Dalai Lama. Neither the United States nor the United Nations did anything but protest. How could they, when India, the chief target, though rudely shaken from its illusion of peaceful coexistence with Red China, was too frightened to take countermeasures and too proud to accept Pakistan's offer of common defense against further Red aggression?

Toward the end of 1958, the emboldened Khrushchev shifted his political offensive back to Europe. To fortify the East German Communists, who had been unable to prevent the exodus to West Germany of millions of discontented subjects, and to reassure Communist Poland and Czechoslovakia, both of which feared a reunited Germany, Khrushchev suddenly demanded that West Berlin be made a "free city" without Western garrisons and information services.

One might have expected an America conscious of its strength and of its rights disdainfully to reject negotiations on anything short of the reunification of all Germany. Eisenhower, in explaining to the American people his acceptance of negotiation, insisted (March 16, 1959) that he would neither give up American rights nor desert the people of West Berlin. But since only a few days before, he had virtually excluded both a nuclear and a "ground war in Europe," he did not impress other governments with American firmness. Nonetheless, Chancellor Adenauer and President de Gaulle opposed concessions.

Prime Minister Macmillan had two reasons for favoring "flexibility." First, he faced "flexible" Socialists at a coming election. Second, piqued by his inability to prevent the formation of a six-power Common Market on the European continent, and alarmed by the progressive intimacy between West Germany and France, he had embarked upon what looked like a campaign to destroy Adenauer. British public opinion, always a generation behind events, had, in the Thirties, feared Stalin when it should have feared Hitler. In the late Fifties it awoke to the possible dangers of (allegedly) renascent German nationalism. A British-

Russian détente leading to better relations between the U.S.S.R. and the U.S.A. might eliminate the trend toward the political and economic unity of the continent. So Macmillan slipped off to Moscow and despite rebuffs from Khrushchev accepted the latter's idea of a new Summit Meeting of the four heads of state (shades of 1955!) at which they would discuss a new status for West Berlin.

The Prime Minister did not destroy Adenauer but during a subsequent visit to Washington, he won the President over to a new Summit Meeting. Dulles, near death, had posed two conditions: Soviet withdrawal of the ultimatum and a successful preliminary conference of foreign ministers. But with Dulles gone, the President's noble ambition of crowning his political life as a peacemaker crowded out the last remnant of Dulles' "bold new program" and the "brinkmanship" of which he had made the mistake of boasting. Despite Russia's intransigence over Berlin at the Geneva Conference, Eisenhower sent Vice President Nixon to Moscow.

Nixon gained the favor of the American people by the way in which he stood up to Khrushchev in an extraordinary argument in the model kitchen of the American exhibit at the Moscow Fair. In private, as judged by the transcript of a long conversation, he behaved more as the bearer of a friendly invitation from the American President to Khrushchev to honor the United States by his presence. In any case, Khrushchev accepted.

His visit was the first act of a tragi-comedy. Whether influenced by Nixon's courtesy or as part of a studied role, the Enemy No. 1 of democracy arrived in a mood of truculence. He had come not to learn but to teach. At every opportunity, he lectured Americans.

To a selected group of "capitalists" at dinner in Averell Harriman's home in New York shortly after his arrival, he expressed his satisfaction at meeting the American "ruling circle" and refused to budge from that view. He declined an invitation to ask questions, apparently feeling that he knew all there was to know. And when David Sarnoff persistently asked why he did not permit freedom of communications between the two countries, he answered surlily: "What you want is freedom for your propaganda to come into our country and we regard that as interference with our internal affairs. We will never allow that."

Replying to a question at the National Press Club in Washington, he snarled that Hungary seemed to stick in some Americans' throats like a dead rat they could neither swallow down nor spit out.

In California, after a public meeting at which he was mildly heckled and a fairly stormy private conversation with American labor leaders, he threatened to go home unless he were treated with the respect which was his due. Whereupon, instead of replying that America was a free country and visitors were free to go or stay, jittery State Department officials asked people please to refrain from provoking him further.

In many places, prominent Americans spontaneously welcomed the sworn enemy of all that their country traditionally stood for, if not like a brother, at least like a very distinguished cousin. The more some Americans made of him, the more he felt he could demand.

During the final stay with the President at Camp David, Maryland, the Butcher of Budapest received an invitation from the ever-genial Eisenhower to call him friend, heard Eisenhower refer to the Berlin situation as "abnormal" (which it certainly was, owing to the Soviet Union's grip on all East Germany) and departed with the impression that at the next Summit Meeting he could expect solid concessions from the West.[9]

In addition to the disarmament negotiations that had been going on fruitlessly for years, the President had, on August 22, 1958, accepted a long-debated Soviet proposal to stop all nuclear tests

[9] See Louis Fischer, *Russia, America and the World.*

by both sides, provided that it could be done under effective supervision. The Republicans had derided this proposal when it was made during the 1956 Presidential campaign by Adlai Stevenson. Following the visit to Moscow of Macmillan early in 1960, while the British were celebrating the "spirit of Camp David," the President wrote an astounding letter to the Soviet Premier. Eisenhower invited Khrushchev to set his mind at rest by assuring him that in the foreseeable future the United States had no intention of sharing atomic secrets with its allies. Why then should the U.S.S.R. need any formal agreement to stop tests or limit membership in the nuclear club?

Further, Eisenhower launched upon a program of the broadest possible cultural exchanges with Communist countries (excepting Red China) and embarked upon a sort of double diplomacy. On the one hand he had recourse ever more frequently to the United Nations despite the ever-lessening influence of the United States within that body owing to the mass entrance of new, nonaligned states.

On the other, he developed the personal diplomacy he had begun with Khrushchev and extended it to all parts of the world. In the last two years of his Administration, Eisenhower made no less than four extended trips outside the United States, thus setting a Presidential precedent. The ovations that he received everywhere he went made him ever more confident of the success of his peace crusade. From this time on, he sought no more allies and avoided further "polarization" of the world, unmoved by the total polarization of the Communist third of mankind.[10] He confidently looked forward to his coming visit to Moscow as a milestone on the path to reconciliation between the hostile camps.

This was not to be. Each sign of Western eagerness for a "relaxa-

[10] The President was reported to have told a Nigerian who visited him in October, 1960, "We are not a bloc. . . . We do not urge, indeed, we do not desire, that you should belong to one camp or the other."

tion of tensions" became just another occasion for the Kremlin to increase them. Khrushchev had, if not misinterpreted, at least over-interpreted, the "spirit of Camp David." As he became aware of his mistake, his anger mounted.

In March, 1960, President de Gaulle of France informed Khrushchev in Paris that despite the courtesy of his French welcome he could expect no further Berlin gains at the coming Summit.

On May 5, Khrushchev revealed that an American spy plane, the U-2, had been shot down a few days previously while deep over Soviet territory. There was nothing surprising in this. For several years American planes had observed Soviet territory from heights where they could not be shot down. Soviet planes were regularly flying over Northern Alaska and Canada. The British Air Force had played a considerable part in the game, which they called "spoofing." It consisted of sending planes over an opponent's defenses and tempting him to reveal them by bringing them into action. "Spoofing" aircraft were equipped with detection instruments that let them know when enemy radar was on them.[11] The pilot of the U-2 either had bad luck or neglected to take necessary precautions and was captured. When the Administration ineptly lied about the flight, Khrushchev revealed that the captured pilot had confessed.

The Soviet chief went to Paris for the planned Summit of May 16 determined to make the most of the incident. He intended, at the least, to compel the American President to apologize publicly as his price for participating in any Big Four meeting. Failing to obtain an apology, he arrogantly torpedoed the very Summit he had worked so hard to bring about.

There was little harm in that. Khrushchev simply had no interest in a Summit at which he could not obtain the internationalization of West Berlin. But before leaving Paris, he convoked in the

[11] See Brigadier General Thomas R. Phillips, U. S. A. (ret.), *The Bulletin of the Atomic Scientists,* June, 1960.

largest hall of the temporary building adjacent to the Palais de Chaillot the largest group of newsmen ever assembled at any international conference to hear him justify his action. Khrushchev sat at a green draped table at one end, Marshal Malinovski, much bemedalled, on his left and Foreign Minister Gromyko on his right. Beyond Gromyko were two Soviet interpreters, one of whom did most of the translating into heavily accented but fluent French and English.

Then began what may have been the strangest press conference of all time. As he arose to read roughly the same tirade he had presented to the three Western statesmen, Nikita was greeted by loud boos. He first grinned at Malinovski, then called the disapprovers "bastards sent by Chancellor Adenauer." He said he regretted that all of them had "not been buried like other Nazis at Stalingrad." Next he read for a few moments in Russian, then stopped suddenly and turned the document over to the interpreter who, first in French and then in English, proceeded inexorably to the end. The tirade contained nothing that had not already been printed.

Finally came the climax—question time. Here the Soviet leader outdid even his own reputation for discourtesy. Accompanied by alternate boos and applause, he bobbed up and down in his chair. Sometimes he spoke softly, his features immobile as those of a Buddha. Occasionally he put on his folksy smile. A few times his voice rose to a strident roar, his generally pale face becoming dark red, his fists clenched and his arms swinging, or pointing a stubby finger at a questioner. And for the first half hour he literally stunned his normally blasé listeners with the crudity of his remarks.

Never in forty years of attendance at major international conferences had I seen or heard such a torrent of official abuse, not even from Adolf Hitler. The German Fuehrer had directed his attacks at the "fourteen years of German slavery and humiliation" allegedly imposed upon his innocent countrymen by the Allies at Versailles, and later carried out by "Jews, Slavs and other subhumans." The Russian "Vozhd" directed his insults at President Eisenhower.

Starting with the unlucky U-2, Nikita cursed his hostile listeners as "lackeys of [American] imperialism." He promised to down any other such American flights and to bomb the non-American airfields from which they took off. He shrieked against U.S. espionage. He labeled Americans pirates, bandits, spies, aggressors, imperialists, provocateurs, fishy friends and cowards. President Eisenhower he called a thief "caught red-handed" and suggested his head be "banged against the wall" as Nikita's mother had punished a cat caught climbing into the pigeon loft. How, Nikita piously asked, could Russians innocent of all espionage sit down to negotiate with such an unrepentant warmonger?

Nikita further applauded the revolution in Cuba and predicted that other Latin-American countries would "revolt," with the approval of the U.S.S.R. He solemnly pledged himself to sign a separate treaty with the East German pseudo-state. He promised his listeners that the Western powers would "be deprived of" their occupation rights in West Berlin.

It was a fascinating and at first a noteworthy performance. Gradually, however, such excessive but monotonous violence palled and newsmen began to lose interest, leave their seats and drift out of the room. Quickly Khrushchev was on his feet in a final bound. He was, he explained, ready to continue answering questions but understandably his Soviet interpreters, claiming that they had put in a full day, were threatening to leave. And thus terminating what had started as a new, more sensational Sputnik and ended as a punctured balloon, Nikita walked from the great hall, while anti-Communists booed and the Communist claque burst into final applause. Even as he disappeared, a gray-haired man in a blue suit was screaming over and over again an unintelligible insult. "A Hungarian refugee," someone explained to an American newsman.

Nikita had got no concession on West Berlin, but he went home with something far more valuable: in his embarrassment at being caught in a lie, Eisenhower told the assembled statesmen at Paris that he *had already called off further flights over Soviet territory.* Yet these flights had been for years the chief source of information about Soviet military targets, and American knowledge of these targets was the essence of the policy of deterrence. No gunner can hit targets he cannot locate. No substitute for the U-2 flights was in sight. Since the Soviets had found a means of shooting them down further flights were conceivably too dangerous. But why tell Khrushchev they had been stopped? Certainly, in renouncing them publicly, the President gave away another diplomatic card as unaccountably as he had, by imprudent statements in 1955 and 1956, eliminated Soviet fear of an American nuclear attack.

From the Paris Summit to the end of his Administration, Eisenhower underwent a series of personal humiliations and diplomatic defeats while Khrushchev's arrogance rose to new heights. In *Pravda* (June 4, 1960) he referred to Eisenhower as fit to run a kindergarten.

On June 16, Communist-inspired rioters in Tokyo, demanding the end of the American alliance, compelled the American President to renounce his long-planned visit to Japan, thereby revealing the depth to which they had implanted the "neutralist" microbe into a great allied people. On June 27, the Soviet delegates insolently stalked out of the unending East-West disarmament conference.

On July 6, a week after Belgium freed the Congo, the Congolese Premier-designate, Patrice Lumumba, captained a conspiracy of African nationalists and miscellaneous fellow-travelers, who raped and murdered Belgians and almost managed to put the Congo into the list of Communist-directed states.

Not surprisingly, Secretary of State Herter reported to Eisenhower that Khrushchev no longer seemed to take the United States seriously, and suggested an increase in the defense budget —to no avail.

On September 19, Nikita and the heads of several satellite states arrived at the United Nations Assembly in New York (whither their visit attracted other international leaders, including Eisenhower, Macmillan, Nasser, Nkrumah, Nehru, Diefenbaker, Menzies, the Crown Prince of Morocco and the King of Jordan) and proceeded to make it the greatest Communist publicity stunt ever seen. His presence, and that of his Communist confreres, blocked New York traffic, totally exhausted the local police force and turned the United Nations Assembly into a circus.

Khrushchev publicly embraced the bearded Castro of Cuba. Like some winsome Juliet, he stood on the balcony of his hotel and exchanged banter with Romeo-like reporters on the sidewalk below. When despite his efforts to captain the new African states, he was unable to have his way in the Congo, he abused Secretary General Hammarskjöld and haughtily demanded the drastic reorganization of the United Nations. Six days later he heckled Macmillan and pounded on his desk with his shoe, a gesture he had been given to believe was an old American custom.[12] All in all, he stole about ninety per cent of the publicity from the other notables present, including Dwight D. Eisenhower.

Then, still muttering threats about West Berlin (which he had promised East Germany's Communist boss Ulbricht would be his "before the cherry trees bloomed again"), about Africa and about the United Nations, he departed as noisily as he had arrived.

He made headlines again toward the end of the year. The Communist Party Meeting at Moscow was the most important ever

[12] Soviet officials present were worried lest their chief be photographed while yawning. See Andrew Boyd, *The Eastern Economist,* New Delhi, November 18, 1960.

held. Representatives of eighty-one Communist Parties attended, with seven absent. After about two weeks of meetings, held in as much secrecy as possible, they issued a statement that was one long boast of past progress and of future triumphs. It set forth undying hostility to capitalism, particularly to the United States, the "mainstay of colonialism today" and the "enemy of the peoples of the entire world." It promised future trouble, even "wars of liberation." Most striking was the evidence it provided that after almost twenty years of efforts at conciliation, the West was farther from true peaceful coexistence than it had ever been.

To make his enmity doubly clear, Nikita went out of his way to announce that he would have nothing more to do with the lame-duck Eisenhower and would insist that Eisenhower's successor return to the "friendly spirit" of Roosevelt. He boasted to the delegates: "Comrades, we live in a splendid time: Communism has become the invincible force of our century."

Why was Khrushchev so confident? Politically the United States had lost influence. Economically it was in trouble. Unemployment was higher than at any time since 1940 and an adverse balance of payments had provoked a flight from the dollar. Moreover, by his failure to accelerate legally ruled racial integration throughout America, Eisenhower had tolerated the continuance of what could become America's greatest handicap in its future dealings with colored peoples. Under his management the relative military power of the United States had steadily deteriorated, though perhaps not as much as his adversaries claimed.

During his tenure of office, imperial Communism had successfully seized North Vietnam, threatened the independence of little Laos, lit a smouldering fire in Africa and crossed the Atlantic into Cuba. Each successive Communist conquest was bringing the West closer to an ultimate choice between war and submission to Moscow. Such a tragic dilemma was surely what Charles

De Gaulle had had in mind when in 1954 he had remarked: "America is Carthage."

This, obviously, was not the way the situation looked to Dwight D. Eisenhower. On January 13, 1961, he sent to Congress a State of the Union message that was an encomium of his own work:

He had kept inflation small. He had prevented the American military establishment from growing to a point where it could menace a free society. And above all, he had kept the peace, "always with honor." He had taken the first steps toward nuclear disarmament and felt confident that with time and patience the West could convert the Soviet rulers from a policy of world conquest to the acceptance of world law.

He had been the most popular American president of all time. Internationally, people had acclaimed him and found his friendly optimism contagious. Reason would prevail in a not too distant future. Why should he not be satisfied, off there at the farm in Gettysburg? God, or the next President, would look after America.

Chapter IX

COMMUNIST ENCIRCLEMENT

"A conqueror is always a lover of peace.... He would like to make his entry into our state unopposed."

—KARL VON CLAUSEWITZ

Back in 1918, shortly after taking power, Lenin outlined one article of what became the credo of all Communists:

"Either the power of the Soviets triumphs in all the world's developed countries or Anglo-Saxon imperialism, the most reactionary, the most furious, the strangler of the small, weak peoples, establishes world-wide reaction. One of the two. No middle ground."

Thirty-odd years later, Nikita Khrushchev informed his rivals of the approaching triumph of the Soviets' power: "We shall bury you."

With some plausibility. For, considered as a unit, the Communist bloc was far closer to world rule than any empire of the past. "Communism," said Charles Malik of Lebanon in 1960, "started from zero forty-three years ago and today it rigidly controls one third of mankind and has penetrated and softened up, in varying degrees, the remaining two thirds." This was something that no

Alexander, Trajan, conquering Arab, Tamerlane, Genghis Khan or Bonaparte had ever even approached. Not even Britain's absent-mindedly acquired empire whereon the sun never set could match the combined Communist-ruled states in area, population or relative power.

"One-third of three billion human beings," as Nikita Khrushchev coldly reminded the United Nations General Assembly (1960), had "established socialist statehood" in the previous fifteen years. (The real figure was about 800 million.) While this growth was occurring, the non-Communist nations of the West more or less willingly relinquished what became thirty-eight new nations with another 800 million inhabitants—with more to come.

Even more significant, freedom and democracy (mislabeled capitalism by Khrushchev) were steadily on the defensive, Communism on the offensive. Where freedom fought back, as in Germany, Korea, Iran, Vietnam, Lebanon, Guatemala it at best succeeded in holding its own. Nowhere did it regain anything into which the Soviet bear had firmly fixed its claws.

To quote again from Charles Malik, "The simple fact that the free world has not succeeded in forty years in pushing back the tide of Communism by one inch from where it really got political control leaves the strong impression that we are dealing here with an irresistible and irreversible thrust which will inevitably inherit and transform in its own image all the kingdoms and cultures of the earth."

Small wonder that many Westerners, with the memory of historical success indelibly fixed in their memories, tried to put such thoughts out of their minds. In the 1960 campaign the American Presidential candidates spent a lot of time arguing about the state of American *prestige*. Neither could deny that in the growth of relative *power*, the Communist world had over the previous years gained on the non-Communists. To the United Nations Khrushchev boasted that since the U.S.S.R.'s strength was "at least equal to that of the United States," if one considered the other "socialist countries," one would conclude that "not only law and justice but [superior] force too" was on the side of the "peace-loving states." Nikita's claim of Soviet power equal to that of the United States was, of course, exaggerated or premature, but undoubtedly the trend had been heavily in Russia's favor.

Indeed, with but brief reverses, it had been in Russia's favor ever since Ivan the Terrible took Kazan in 1552. In terms of territorial expansion, Russian history as a whole was a success story that far surpassed that of the United States. It began—some would say typically—with a betrayal of the West. The great Mongol tide that swept over East Europe submerged and destroyed most of the existing states in what later became Russia. The small (68,000-square-mile) Duchy of Moscow survived and prospered by becoming first the obsequious vassal and then the *ally* of its Asian conquerors. Nor is it without interest to note that in allying himself with Red China, Stalin repeated what Russian rulers had done with the great Khans centuries before. Machiavellian Dukes of Moscow had in a sense anticipated the Georgian autocrat.

After 1552, Russian rule spread like an epidemic. North to the Baltic and the Arctic Ocean, west to Prussia, southwest almost to Byzantium, south to the Black Sea, Turkey and Iran, southeast to Afghanistan, India and Tibet, but most of all east and northeast to China, Mongolia, the Sea of Japan, the Sea of Okhotsk, the Pacific Ocean, Russian explorers, trappers and soldiers pressed forward. They spilled over the Bering Strait into North America with results that would today be incalculable, if a shortsighted nineteenth-century czar had not been foolish enough in 1867 to sell Alaska to the United States for a song.

In 1917, despite a serious repulse in the 1904-05 war with Japan, the Russian empire was in territory the largest in the world and in population the largest in Europe. Certainly, few conquerors were less welcome. Several subject peoples took advantage of the

Bolshevik revolution to break away from Russian rule. Lenin temporarily recognized the right of secession of all non-Russian peoples (and the Soviet Constitution of 1936 roughly confirmed this right), but as soon as he overcame the badly led and worse supported Whites, he reconquered most of the "rebellious" provinces of the former empire. Thereafter, while Soviet rulers continued to affirm the right of secession (Khrushchev on American television in October, 1960), they actually considered any attempt to secede tantamount to "capitalist treason" and punished it accordingly.

Once he had overcome and exiled his arch-rival, the internationalist Leon Trotsky, Stalin concentrated on making the U. S. S. R. a worthy successor of the czarist empire, even rehabilitating the reputation of Ivan the Terrible. It was soon apparent that far from having abolished imperial and colonial exploitation, the Red czars in the Kremlin were planning the greatest colonial empire ever dreamed by man. The form had changed; the substance remained.

Russian boyars, grand dukes, and court favorites gave way to Communist Party bosses, functionaries and secret police, to whom were gradually added a sprinkling of trade and industrial managers, tame intellectuals and other members of the new ruling elite. But real power remained with the party (called by Charles Malik "the most superbly organized international political party in history") under which the Soviet state became the merest administration.

Yet until World War Two, which he helped to trigger, Stalin had to be patient. For earlier, when Soviet Communism had virtually declared war on all non-Communist governments, the latter had retorted by encasing the Soviet Empire within the *cordon sanitaire* that prevented any immediate spread of Red rule. So the Kremlin bided its time, meanwhile perfecting its organization abroad and its brain laundries at home.

Opportunity came with the second war between "capitalist

imperialist countries" (which Communist leaders had predicted). The drive for an all-Red world state was on.

By the end of 1960, the Communist bloc exercised control or preponderant influence over seventeen countries and parts of eight others. Beyond the "heartland" extending from the Bering Strait to approximately the Lübeck-Trieste line in Europe, and south into India, it had established bridgeheads in West Africa and the Caribbean. Moreover, by accepting Lenin's great plan of wholeheartedly encouraging the "bourgeois-nationalist-revolutionary elements in the Western colonies," Khrushchev and Mao not only gained popularity and prestige in the newly liberated states but in Latin-America, the Middle East and Southeast Asia. They had outflanked the Western "containment lines" and were successfully spreading their enticing poison to other "enemy" countries.

So much was obvious, but Mr. K. and Mr. Mao had still more to gloat over. Despite the fifteen-years shrinkage of Communist Party membership in most capitalist lands, Communism held its own or better in countries like Italy and Greece, was gaining in Japan and throughout Latin-America, and remained dangerously strong in France. Moreover, by seeming to seek greater influence for the growing number of non-aligned members of the United Nations, the U.S.S.R. could hope to direct that once overwhelmingly anti-Communist world organization.

At home, by efficient brain-washing and stern repression, the U.S.S.R. and Red China had, at least for the time, broken any incipient will to revolt. Mao Tse-tung had murdered domestic opponents on a scale even surpassing the U.S.S.R., and later, by the "hundred flowers" trick, eliminated his discontented intellectuals.

To prevent the anti-colonialism it fostered from spreading to its own conglomerate populations (about forty-eight per cent non-Russian, divided into fifty-nine major groups), the Kremlin had embarked upon a process of scrambling these peoples by infiltration and deportation. Balts, Tartars, Volga Germans and Chechen-Ingush citizens were moved or dispersed and young Ukrainians were successfully "encouraged" to colonize the "virgin lands" of remote Siberia. Meanwhile, Russians in increasing numbers moved into the Ukraine and the Moslem "federal republics." The Kremlin disenfranchised Jews as a people, deprived them of important jobs, treated them as aliens—yet forbade them to emigrate.

Much of this not only strengthened the tyranny but was successfully camouflaged from foreign eyes.

For several years after 1945, the war-devastated and shaky U.S.S.R. "milked" the equally devastated European satellite peoples by the process of buying from them cheap and selling to them dear. This was part of the frantic rush to rebuild its own military power before the "capitalists" could catch on and take advantage of its weakness. But there had been little danger of that. Communists erroneously attributed to their intended victims an aggressiveness equal to their own.

Once sufficiently recovered, the U.S.S.R. took up the American challenge of giving economic and technical aid to newly independent and neutral peoples. Lenin had predicted (*Pravda*, March 4, 1923) that the "outcome of the struggle depends in the long run on the fact that Russia, India and China form most of the population of the globe." With China already Red and India in the hands of pacifist Socialists, Communism's chances of eventually subverting the entire undecided third of mankind seemed bright. Between late 1954 and June, 1959, the Communist bloc granted or loaned some four billion dollars in direct aid to some twenty non-aligned countries, and to them only. In addition, over the same fifty-two months, the Communist countries supplied about 6,900 economic technicians, sixty-five per cent of them Russian, to twenty-three countries. Communist aid remained insignificant in comparison to American. But whereas a considerable part of American aid was humanitarian and "tranquilizing," Communist assistance was skillfully applied to specific spots for specific ends—to encourage sympathy for the U.S.S.R. and Red China, nourish Communist Parties, and prepare an eventual take-over.

Red aid was, moreover, more successful than the limited amount might indicate. *Pravda* (August, 1960) noted gleefully that "peaceful coexistence was not impeding national liberation movements" (the understatement of the year) and through one Georgi M. Zhukov, boasted that "transition of a non-capitalist way of development" would come "as soon as vital national programs" were "achieved."[1]

The sober truth was that the growth of Communist power, influence and naked dominion surpassed anything that either Lenin or Stalin had foreseen. At the end of the war, Stalin had mendaciously sworn his lack of interest in spreading Soviet Communism to the conquered European satellites, to Greece or to China. He had done so, not because he had no such interest—it was his dearest goal. However, he could not believe that the United States would not fight to stop him. Only after he became convinced that American leaders would protest but not act did he move quickly. Thus, when the Truman Administration disclaimed direct military interest in South Korea and Formosa, he moved immediately to have Korea attacked and would have embarked Red China on an attack on Formosa as well, had not the outrage in Korea compelled sluggish American generals to revise their estimate of the island's strategic value.

Not all the uproar over the Hungarian revolt prevented the neutral world's respect for Soviet power from rising sharply. For people everywhere could not but contrast the U.S.S.R.'s brutal

[1] The status of Communism in most parts of the world in mid-1960 was ably described by Frank Gibney in *The Khrushchev Pattern*. Duell, Sloan and Pearce, New York, 1960.

effectiveness in Hungary with American passivity in the face of the heroic struggle of Hungarians, Poles and East Germans.

In fact, in the first seven years after Stalin's death, Nikita Khrushchev raised the Soviet Union from a poor second to a dangerous rival of the United States. Meanwhile, Mao had occupied Tibet and subdued the stiff-necked Tibetans by genocide and had taken the mountain passes leading into India. How had China developed such force on its inferior economic and industrial bases?

One chief answer lay in the intense devotion to peace of the major democratic peoples. This was notable everywhere, but most pronounced among Americans—an economically almost sated people who had never been willing to understand or even condone the "power politics" inherent in a world of sovereign nations.[2]

A second reason lay in America's awareness of the appalling destructive power of nuclear weapons. (Biological and chemical weapons were probably equally murderous but for some reason never caught the popular imagination, conceivably because no nation seriously thought of using them except in reprisal.) The well-advertised effects of H-bombs had for the first time in human history made the prospect of war both "unthinkable" and obsessive.

A third basic reason was the inability of the non-Communist peoples to recognize, or perhaps to admit to themselves, the essential nature and full dimensions of the Communist threat.

Still a fourth reason was the Communists' unrivalled skill in taking advantage of every weakness of their opponents and intended victims.

A final cause was Communism's innate appeal to peoples too

[2] Thus the otherwise intelligent David Riesman babbled of "the ulcer of the cold war which exposes the failure of a style of life." Did he prefer it hot?

inexperienced or too intellectually vain to see the barb in the bait and the West's unwillingness to apply the brutal, Communist-type coercive measures that would have kept the colonies in bondage. Each of the five reasons played a major role in Khrushchev's and Mao's successes. Each reason, undoubtedly, helped Western leaders to shut their minds to the fact that Communism was, for the time being at least, persistently Communistic.

A few leaders, like the astute Charles Malik, might recognize the situation as a "life-and-death struggle between international communism . . . and *the rest of the world,* especially the Western world, and in the Western world especially the United States of America."

But President Eisenhower insisted that the United States was not "hostile" to Communism, and refused to accept the challenge; or play to win. Since other Western leaders also refused, Communist imperialism in the nuclear age confronted decent men everywhere with what looked like a choice among a limited number of courses: total or piecemeal surrender; nuclear destruction (of just what and how much nobody could be sure); and a cautious combination of (not too much) deterrent strength with a patient search for conciliation with the enemy.

A fourth course—mustering preponderant collective strength and wearing down and outlasting the adversary—was open and promising, but it demanded imagination, radical new policies, persistent determination and higher taxes. Those Westerners who suggested it were met, if not silenced, by the charge that they were "risking all-out war" and few in government discussed their proposal seriously.

Yet only the softest of Westerners were, even by 1961, ready for surrender to Communism. They were, however, even less ready for nuclear war and trusted that their adversaries shared their repugnance. There remained open only the third course of maintaining a minimum deterrent force, seeking no real unity of strategy among the chief non-Communist nations (lest Communists consider it a "provocation"), taking Khrushchev's talk of peaceful coexistence literally and seeking, through negotiation on almost anything, to bring about that "relaxation of tensions" and disarmament which could remove the danger of nuclear war and perhaps lead, step by step, to a "better understanding."[3]

This policy of waiting for something to turn up could, however, succeed only if the Communists renounced their goal of world rule. But to do so, they must either be threatened with war by a manifestly superior force or otherwise compelled to recognize the vanity of their worldwide ambition. On the other hand, once they understood that they were in no danger of being attacked, they were free to keep everything they possessed, strive for more by all means short of major war; and, meanwhile, hope to equal or even surpass their combined but sluggish adversaries in military power. In short, *they no longer had any reason to consider negotiation as more than a device to gain time in which to divide, immobilize and demoralize their opponents.*

Small wonder that Mr. Khrushchev publicly exuded satisfaction even in the face of minor setbacks. There was indeed something fantastic about European peoples who had so lately paid an awful penalty for their refusal to take Adolf Hitler at his word still refusing to believe Nikita. Yet they did refuse. So did many Americans.

Instead of facing up to the grim reality, the "most powerful country in the world" (to quote its President) developed a movie debutante's sensitivity to what it chose to call "world public opinion"[4] regardless of the teaching of history (and of General MacArthur) that in international affairs there is no substitute for success.

[3] This program was the essence of President Eisenhower's Farewell Address.
[4] Defined by a British politician, Mark Bonham Carter, as "the last refuge of any politician with no opinion of his own."

A complicating factor (as I noted earlier) was the new explosion of national self-determination. The idea went back centuries. But given powerful expression by Woodrow Wilson, revived by Presidents Roosevelt and Truman, accepted by President Eisenhower, it came to mean that what was good for Americans was good for Berbers, Congolese, Laotians and the naked Nagas of India. Thus at the time when the powerful states were moving toward integration into larger units, the weakest and less developed were claiming an absolute independence which they lacked the military means to defend and the economic means to support, and further were insisting that through the United Nations, which they dominated numerically, their influence and desires be made paramount. Even when confronted with the awful example of the liberated Belgian Congo, few Americans saw the absurdity of such claims.

In fact, not content with relinquishing these one-time elements of their own camp, many Americans positively urged the liberated states to seek international "non-alignment" rather than remain allied with their former masters. It was reasoned that the new states "naturally" wished to stay outside opposing "power blocs" and as neutrals would better oppose Communism than if they became "unwilling allies." A leading British newspaper correspondent even argued that increasing non-alignment might be the road back from power politics to "sanity."

Lenin had been right. Colonies and a bad conscience were the Achilles' heel of the West. Premature colonial emancipation subjected a mass of largely illiterate, culturally backward peoples to the full pressure of Communist propaganda, flattery, subversion, and military threats.

And the fact was that to Western-trained and madly ambitious leaders of peoples barely emerging from tribal savagery, Communism's program of "institutional centralism" (tyranny to you) and controlled mass movement and opinion was more attractive than the personal freedom advocated by the West. In consequence, as Lenin had foreseen, premature national independence was the gateway to a path that could lead through non-alignment to full Communist take-over.

In addition, many Westerners really believed that higher living standards would better protect "underdeveloped" peoples from Communism than any number of intercontinental ballistic missiles. Like President Eisenhower, they saw the Soviet challenge as basically a competition in economic productivity.

Another group of Westerners, seeking an alternative to the Cold War, put their primary trust in promoting more democracy everywhere. They were ready to wash their hands of "corrupt and undemocratic" foreign regimes, such as those of Chiang Kai-shek in China, Syngman Rhee of Korea and Batista of Cuba (none of which could possibly harm the United States), and if the alternatives were Communist regimes, well, at least the Communists "did something for the people."

A few such Americans never forgave Truman for accepting Dictator Franco of Spain as an ally, although they approved massive aid to the national Communist Tito of Yugoslavia and to the orthodox Communist Gomulka of Poland. Nor were these Americans disturbed by Khrushchev's cheerful willingness to support capitalist rulers anywhere provided they were anti-American.

This group further insisted that to oppose Communism successfully in Laos or Buganda Americans must show "clean hands at home." It was, of course, true that persisting racial discrimination in the American South, pointed up by occasional insults to dark-skinned visiting diplomats, gave Communists an unfailing propaganda weapon against the United States. But American reformers did not stop with a demand for desegregation a century overdue. Some wanted nothing less than a great religious revival. Moral Re-Armament spokesmen argued that, to combat the effective communist "ideology," peoples everywhere needed conversion to "absolute honesty and absolute purity." Now a Western civilization increasingly corroded by materialism, violence and atrocious taste offered room for Moral Re-Armament. The "morally rearmed" were immune to all forms of Communist subversion. But how a community of saints would have successfully resisted the Communist combination of violence and deceit remained to be explained.

These Western reformers were honest in their efforts, however confusing the result. But there was worse. As Communism acquired greater power and influence, other Americans found hitherto unsuspected virtue in it as a system. The Hungarian-born John Lukacs felt able to equate the desires of the peoples of Hawaii and Alaska to join the United States with the seizure of neighboring countries by the Soviets, as parallel cases of imperialism. Certain American scientists, eager to eliminate the awful atomic threat which they had brought upon mankind, continually summoned the world to disarm or die.[5] They sought continuing contact and consultation with their Soviet counterparts in the search for understanding. They chose to overlook the fact that, in Soviet society, scientists were either politically powerless or the willing tools of the Communist conspiracy.

Even less did these Americans perceive that precisely because major war had become unthinkable, the "stalemate of terror" opened to Communist leaders an endless opportunity for brinkmanship, with the prize going to the boldest brinkman. For if the adversary refused disarmament on Western terms, or to accept a compromise, then logically the West would have no alternative but to accept his.

[5] The British scientist and novelist, Sir Charles Percy Snow, had the unscientific effrontery to tell a scientific gathering that no sane man could hesitate between unpoliced disarmament and sure destruction.

American foreign policy was, indeed, heavily influenced by all sorts of professors who imagined that costly surveys and analyses, endless reports by study committees and "scientific re-examinations of situations" could replace the statesman's genius for cutting through to and acting on the major issue. Some sociologists went even further, proclaiming that in the "new era" of nuclear weapons, humans "would have" to develop an entirely new behavior pattern. Others were unable to make up their minds.

Anyhow, the thing to do was to keep on negotiating about almost anything since "governments that talk do not fight." (This was, by the way, a complete reversal of the truth. A government that was planning a nuclear attack could not do better than to schedule it during a conference on disarmament or peaceful coexistence.) Such argument was all of a piece with the line that urged American diplomatic recognition of Red China and its admission to the United Nations as a natural concession to the nation's size and slowly mounting strength.

During Mr. K.'s truculent tour of the United States in 1959, groups of industrialists and bankers suddenly "discovered" that perhaps they could do business with Communism. A Wall Street scribe wrote that "the new leaders of American politics do not have the same emotional dislike of Communism as the old leaders had." A Canadian-born tycoon, one Cyrus Eaton, positively fawned on the Ukrainian murderer. A year later, softhearted Eleanor Roosevelt saw no reason not to "pursue peace" by receiving the arch-enemy of her country.

Still another product of the times was a professor of theology who, in a little volume, *Christianity and Communism Today*, while admitting that the Administration "had a right to" prevent the spread of Communism and avoid a third world war, urged Christians to "accept" Communism in both Red Russia and Red China and recognize that "both nations have legitimate interests."

Americans should, he argued, refrain from trying to overthrow or provoke two regimes not only barbarous in themselves but bent on destroying them. The author could see little or no difference between the U.S.S.R. and the U.S.A. "There are," he wrote, "aggressors, big bosses and little bosses in all countries." [6]

Other pious Western Christians, who fifteen years before felt no overweening urge to pay heavy taxes in order to help Indians or Hottentots, suddenly discovered that such help was not politically expedient (which could be argued) but an ethical imperative.[7]

Yet another Communist trump was the Westerners' inability to agree upon the nature of the enemy. Some said it was Communism; others said it was aggression. To say that it was Communism implied that the United States should seek the downfall of all Communist regimes, whether or not linked to the U.S.S.R. If aggression, then, by this reasoning, joining the U.S.S.R. to prevent Britain, France and Israel from crushing Nasser's Egypt had been a great American triumph, no matter how much it weakened the major American alliance.

As a result, in all Western and non-aligned countries, publicists who had unceasingly aroused their countrymen against Fascism saw no reason to be overly alarmed by Communist infiltration. Behind this particular confusion was the growing realization of the need for peace to preserve civilization. The obvious alternative to national violence was enforceable world law.

Because the United States, by remaining aloof from the League of Nations, had perhaps contributed to bringing on World War

[6] A good number accepted this "image" theory—the U.S.S.R. and the U.S.A. as increasingly "similar" societies.

[7] Edmond Stillman and William Pfaff (*Harper's Magazine*, January, 1961) contended "that we should drop any presumption of a righteous crusade against aggressive communism" and save ourselves by curing the "deep personal alienation which today infects our society."

Two, many Americans felt that their country's respect for the Charter of the United Nations should be absolute, barring the use of force except at the request of the international organization or in sheer self-defense. If the U.S.S.R. (as in Hungary) or Red China (as in Korea) practiced aggression, that was no excuse for the United States or its allies to launch counteroffensives. The thing was to establish the habit of substituting peaceful methods for force. If this meant that the United States and the United Nations must look on helplessly while Soviet tanks crushed East Germans, Poles and Hungarians, well, that was part of the price that had to be paid for a world without war.

Yet in a struggle in which one side used armed force whenever it dared and the other used it only in self-defense, the aggressor seemed almost certain to win. Pure defense has never yet won a war.[8] Nor has any successful aggressor ever yet called off a struggle. The awful fact of 1961 was that the primary enemy of free humanity was not aggression in the abstract, or lack of democracy, or poverty or colonialism or corruption or even nuclear weapons but the billion-strong Communist bloc.

The West's (chiefly America's) unwillingness to accept this fact gave Khrushchev and Mao their great opportunity. These leaders enormously stepped up the traditional Communist methods of promoting expansion by subversion, the use of front organizations, social disorders, the backing of liberal causes, the duping of doctrinaire reformers and the tender-hearted, and the infiltration of labor unions and other organizations.

Khrushchev, in particular, raised to a high art the techniques for dividing and paralyzing his major adversaries. This he accom-

[8] In testimony before the Senate Armed Services and Foreign Relations Committees, General George Marshall argued that Wellington had won the Peninsula Campaign in Spain by pure defense. He never mentioned the persistent guerrilla offensives of the Spanish people behind Bonaparte's lines.

plished primarily by playing alternately upon their hope of peace and fear of war. Had not Pavlov demonstrated that dogs could be totally subdued by a skillful mixture of relief and fear? [9]

Stalin, before his death, perceived the advantage of reviving Lenin's offer of "peaceful coexistence" to those whom the U.S.S.R. intended to destroy. He invented the famous Stockholm Peace Pledge, which duped millions of earnest individuals, particularly in the non-aligned nations. Khrushchev went further, raising the peace mirage to a major weapon. He proclaimed it in and out of season as Soviet policy. He backed it by offers to stop nuclear tests. Later he proposed partial disarmament, and then immediate and total disarmament. He did not hide—he could not, there had been too many public revelations—the fact that the peaceful competition he sought implied no retreat on his part but a steady retreat by the West until Communism dominated the world. But he played this aspect down and covered it by emphasis on the relaxation of those very "tensions" which it was an important part of his plan to create.

Nor did Khrushchev concede that the total disarmament which he advocated would have to be based largely on trust, or that he insisted on beginning with the elimination of such elements as overseas bases and nuclear weapons wherein, despite his superior rocketry, he remained inferior. Still less would he admit that any disarmament would have to leave each Communist country with a conventional force large enough to maintain the needed iron discipline over its unhappy population. But he preached total disarmament in and out of season, and it appealed to all who accepted the view that war, not Communism, was the greater danger.

Even so, on no less than forty occasions from 1956 to 1961,

[9] The always perceptive British cartoonist, David Low, published late in 1960 a drawing of four Western leaders as dogs drooling to the sound of a dinner bell rung by Mr. K., their trainer.

Khrushchev or some colleague punctuated this peace campaign with threats of nuclear destruction of one or another of some fifteen countries. Sometimes the threat was merely hinted in polite diplomatic notes; other times it was expressed in the most violent terms. What the Soviet Premier sought was to convince both neutrals and adversaries that the choice of peace or victorious war lay not in *their* hands but in *his;* that he preferred peace to war, but that his patience was not endless.

To demonstrate his seizure of the initiative he pushed a series of unacceptable demands at Berlin, stirred up a successfully disguised Communist rebellion in Cuba, planned Communist uprisings in Asia, Africa and Latin-America, and underlined his impatience by ever more vociferous demands for more Summit Meetings. He made no bones of the fact that at each such meeting he would expect to be paid off handsomely.

Meanwhile, in Russia, China and the satellite countries, military staffs coldly laid plans for future war. Soviet Navy Captain Third Class (commander) Nikolai Fedorovitch Artamonov, a defector from the Communist paradise, attested that preparations for the sneak nuclear destruction of the United States would be carried out whenever the Kremlin decided it could win in one stroke, without fear of nuclear reprisal. West German authorities laid hands on a raft of telltale posters to be put up in a conquered West Germany by conquering East German Communists! Red Chinese officials "leaked" a claim of having several nuclear reactors already in operation—with nuclear missiles soon to follow.

At the same time Khrushchev's exhibitions of crude military power and rapidly growing scientific capacity tended to drive the Western allies apart. Europeans, whose suffering in World War Two predisposed them to peace, shuddered at taking any risk of major war over Korea, Indo-China, Laos or the Congo. American legalism inhibited action at Suez and intervention in Hungary when Europe seemed ready to take a risk.

Western politicians, in short, clung pathetically to the hope of a cheap and easy out. In general the democratic peoples, with the taste of economic plenty in their mouths, resisted suggestions to divert their growing prosperity into an adequate military effort. They further accepted the Communist thesis that Communism could properly keep whatever it had acquired, while everything outside the Communist boundaries was a proper subject for discussion as to "whether or not it should be 'liberated' into a condition more suitable for communist absorption.[10]

Instead of meeting offensive with counteroffensive, free world experts continued to invent ever more fantastic theories explaining why Communism could not win. Among these, starting at the beginning, were: its inherent inefficiency; the resurgence of Russian national feeling; Lenin's reversion to capitalism (the New Economic Policy); Stalin's proclamation of socialism in one country; the discovery that Chinese Communists were only agrarian reformers; Tito's showing the way to national Communism; the increasing influence of the only "nominally Communist" Red Army inside the U.S.S.R.; the softening effect of growing Russian prosperity; the U.S.S.R.'s coming need of the West against the growing rival power of Red China; in fact, anything to prove that no all-out Western effort was necessary.

Essentially the Western peoples, and the non-aligned as well, stuck to their dream of a world in which the bear and the dragon, the bleating calf and the trembling rabbit, would lie down together and in which the Secretary General of the United Nations would lead them.

That dream was necessary if humanity were ultimately to escape the tragic result of its own amoral cleverness. But meanwhile the supreme brinkman went from success to success.

And in consequence, what John Foster Dulles had propheti-

[10] Professor David N. Rowe.

cally if prematurely written of in 1950 in his *War or Peace* and as Secretary of State had been unable to prevent, was coming to pass: capitalist encirclement of Communism was slowly becoming Communist encirclement of capitalism.

Chapter X

"WHEN SHRIMP LEARN TO WHISTLE"

"Everyone should understand . . . that the historic process is irreversible."

—NIKITA KHRUSHCHEV

Roosevelt, Truman and Eisenhower placed their faith in Heraclitus' dictum: *panta rei*—all things flow, including the U.S.S.R. Roosevelt counted on friendship to do the trick; Truman, on containment; Eisenhower, on friendship, containment, more time and an inevitable falling out between the two Red giants, China and Russia. Each President in turn believed that if he could only avoid major war long enough, he could outsit Communist imperialism and get the world back to normal. Just as Marx had predicted—that under international Communism the state would "wither away"—Western leaders hoped that with time and greater prosperity, Communism itself would "wither away." So why "provoke" the provocative Communists, or take "excessive risks"?

Shortly after Stalin's death, Churchill suggested that internal prosperity had supplanted external conquest as the chief Soviet goal. Premier Mendès-France, not to be outdone in optimism, announced that the new rulers in Moscow had "shifted the center of gravity of their efforts to the economic and social fields."

Therefore no need to spend ever vaster sums in keeping ahead of the Soviets in arms. No reason to bother about the new states' growing yen for non-alignment or carp at the "pink" blush on the cheek of some of them. A web of alliances, two fleets permanently overseas—these would suffice. No need even to take too seriously Red Russia's missile threats or Red China's hate-filled ravings. Let the West just be "flexible" and all would end well without a too disturbing effort.

Belief in the withering away of Communist imperialism was comforting, but how credible was it? Opinions differed and nowhere more than among those Western Kremlinologists and professional soothsayers who discovered political intentions behind each Communist text or casual remark and foretold the future of Communism by inspecting the quivering entrails of the victim countries.

To be sure, no observer of Soviet affairs could doubt that the Russia of 1961 was not that of 1951. The thaw, in many respects, was real.

Most spectacular was the relaxation of the terror, a term that covered both the bloody purges of party leaders and the systematic intimidation of the entire people. In 1937 I brought back from Moscow a list of some 150 persons who had been members of the Central Committee. Their fates read like a schoolbook list of Henry VIII's wives—"divorced, beheaded, died." A later account of political cannibalism since 1936 reported: of eleven Cabinet Ministers, nine had been shot; of seven Presidents of the Central Executive Committee of the Russian Communist Party, five had mysteriously "died"; of fifty-three high party officials, forty-three had been executed; of the twenty-three top Communists who drafted the Constitution of 1936, fifteen had been shot; of eighty members of the Supreme Council, seventy had been executed, and of five marshals of the Soviet army, three had been shot as spies or traitors.[1] The list of mere subjects murdered, worked to death or imprisoned ran into the tens of millions.

With Stalin's death, this changed. After executing the bloodthirsty Beria, his successors were satisfied to dismiss, demote or exile their rivals. In fact, in 1956, Khrushchev publicly denounced Stalin's ferocity. First Malenkov and later Khrushchev (for a while) remained merely first in the ruling committee. Later, Khrushchev emerged on top and by 1961 was himself a milder example of the sort of personal rule he had denounced in Stalin.

The thaw also saw the drastic reduction of police powers. While failing to restore normal civil rights (which Russians had never enjoyed except for a few months under Kerensky) the new rulers curbed the power of the secret political police to arrest, torture, imprison, deport and execute without trial. They applied a new penal code and improved prison conditions. After revolts in remote labor camps, they released hundreds of thousands, perhaps millions, of inmates. These infamous places were transformed into "correctional centers," and became somewhat more humane.

From the peasants on cooperative and state farms the leaders no longer demanded compulsory deliveries or fixed quantities of food, although they paid a minimum price.

Despite the infamous "work books," without which nobody could get a job, workers began changing jobs with only economic and social penalties. On the other hand, when Khrushchev decided to cultivate the virgin lands in the east, Komsomols used compulsion in recruiting thousands of young men in both the U.S.S.R. and the satellite countries to settle the new frontier. Khrushchev explained that without some compulsion, the settlement might have "taken fifteen years." On the other hand, many who did not find the job to their liking were permitted to return

[1] *The London Times,* May 30, 1960.

home without penalties. Some of those who remained on the job received bonuses.

Malenkov and Khrushchev also relaxed the thought-control previously exercised on scientists, professors, artists and writers. The publication of Dudintsev's novel, *Not By Bread Alone,* and Boris Pasternak's immunity to arrest after his novel, *Doctor Zhivago,* was published abroad, though belied by the later arrest of his closest professional associate, marked the change of climate.

The regime largely ceased to discriminate against children of aristocratic or bourgeois origins in favor of the offspring of workers and peasants. While continuing to explain growing "hooliganism" and persisting prostitution as "harmful survivals of the past," Soviet courts proceeded more humanely, even imposing suspended sentences. Specially constituted courts handled borderline cases such as drunkenness. Religious cults, though still forbidden to engage in social or artistic endeavors, enjoyed slightly more freedom.

With more liberty for all—especially with the possibility of some free discussion without danger of denunciation and punishment—came a most welcome increase of consumer goods in the cities. Under Stalin at least fifty per cent of the gross national product had gone into reinvestment and armament. Malenkov began a considerable shift to consumer goods. Merchandise never or rarely seen before began to appear in shop windows.

The change in relations with foreigners was equally conspicuous. The U.S.S.R. not only once more welcomed tourists but permitted them to travel—under inspection, of course—to most parts of the country. It invited thousands of foreign students to Russian and satellite universities. It embarked upon scientific and artistic exchanges with capitalist countries. To be sure, Soviet subjects permitted to consort with foreigners at home or abroad were carefully picked for dependability and coached for performance. So were those Russian "officials for science" who met to discuss intellectual and scientific-political questions (the stopping of atomic tests, disarmament techniques) with foreigners. Inside Russia, a group of attractive young women were charged with the seduction and defection of promising foreigners. But it sometimes worked the other way.

Almost startling was the change in diplomatic manners. Breaking down their former rigid seclusion, the new Soviet leaders began to receive foreign diplomats and newsmen, in almost the same way as was routine in other countries. (Stalin had kept so aloof that many ambassadors in Moscow never saw him.) Malenkov, in 1953, started off by dropping the Russian demands for one quarter of Turkey. Then he went on to restore Porkkala to Finland, seek reconciliation with Yugoslavia, resume diplomatic relations with West Germany, negotiate a peace treaty with Japan, open new negotiations with the West on disarmament, press for a ban on further nuclear tests and, finally, accept a peace treaty for Austria.

Years before Eisenhower started traveling, Khrushchev and Bulganin launched a new era of personal diplomacy by visiting India, Burma and Afghanistan. Later they journeyed to other countries. Lenin had sturdily maintained that "history shows us that peace is a truce between wars, war the means of obtaining a little better peace." Khrushchev, in 1955, embarked on a campaign of "revisionism" (hitherto almost the worst crime known to orthodox Leninism) by proclaiming that war was not "inevitable," provided, of course, that capitalist countries submitted to history without fighting.

Most significant of the post-Stalin changes was perhaps the new attitude toward the satellite countries. Trotsky had considered the Russian revolution as the first step in worldwide Communist upheaval. Lenin and Stalin, hemmed behind the *cordon sanitaire*, proclaimed "socialism in one country" as their goal.[2] They treated other Communist countries, and Communists in bourgeois countries, simply as tools of Soviet foreign policy.[3] Stalin exhumed and whitewashed previous Russian tyrants, including Ivan the Terrible.

This gambit paid big dividends during World War Two. Soldiers who would not have given a smile to Communism died magnificently for Mother Russia. Later Stalin continued the same pattern by ruthlessly plundering both the satellite countries and occupied Manchuria in order to restore Russia's economy and power. Until his death, he practiced nationalism, whatever his ultimate intentions. Khrushchev slowly changed this. After the satellite revolts, he fought desperately against "national Communism," and, as protection against its spread, sought economic integration with the neighboring Communist countries. He repeated Stalin's fairy tale (embodied in the 1936 constitution) that any Soviet republic could secede at will. In January, 1961, he told the Central Committee that the "Communist Party of the Soviet Union does not lead other parties. There is no superior or subordinate party in the communist movement." And to prove his sincerity, he renewed his 1956 statement that there were "many paths to socialism."

Some foreigners took him at face value. Thus, after a trip to Russia in 1959, George Steiner told B. B. C. audiences that the "fundamental break with the Russian past did not take place in 1917 . . . [but] after the death of Stalin."

And to the long-suffering Russians, these changes were pretty

[2] Some specialists considered this a blind against further intervention by outside countries while the U.S.S.R. was still weak.

[3] In 1936, German Communist refugees from Hitler found themselves treated in Russia as third-class citizens. A group of Austrians finally sought refuge in the (anti-Communist) Austrian Embassy in Moscow, explaining that they preferred to go home and face trial rather than remain longer in the "Soviet Paradise."

wonderful. In fact, the poet, Alexander Tvardovsky, expressed their gratitude in a poem, *So It Was in the Land:*

> *"In different places*
> *I have noticed: people have become kinder*
> *And softer to each other."*

What the Russian people wanted from the second revolution, according to the experienced and perceptive Louis Fischer, was "to hold all they had and get more," ultimately catching up with the Americans, whose admiration they persistently sought. And nobody could deny that under Khrushchev they were enjoying more consumer goods, or that the elite was living it up even more, or that a few intellectuals, despite their favored treatment, were beginning publicly to question the ritual and the restraints, if not the sacred doctrine, of Marxism-Leninism.

Some Western students of Communist society began to feel that the "taming" of the Soviets (if not of Red China) was coming in one or both of two ways: either through mass *embourgeoisement* as living standards rose; or through the progressive fading or transformation of the ideological conviction of the leaders. Since they claimed to see evidence of both, these students felt that the "patient" Western governments were on the right track.

In fact, President Ayub Khan of Pakistan predicted to me (June, 1960) that Khrushchev must either soon curb the living standard (and the sprouting private lives) of the better paid subjects or see them turn away from Communism. Milovan Djilas stated flatly that Communism could not "liberalize itself" without ceasing to be Communism.

Khrushchev also seemed fully aware of the danger, for he soon took measures to reduce the individual income differential between the top one per cent and the lowest sixty per cent of the population, which stood, in 1957, at a ratio of about sixteen to one. He also changed the educational system to prevent a further widening of the split between mind and hand workers, and held up to public criticism the pampered *stilyagi*, many of them sons of the Soviet elite, who aped foreign youths. Furthermore, after a first visit to Red China, he again stressed heavy industry at some sacrifice of Malenkov's program of more consumer goods. (This was probably the result of a Chinese warning that without speedy industrialization Communist China could not feed its people. And if Mao went, how long would Khrushchev last?) Finally, after revolts in labor camps and outlying districts in the U.S.S.R.[4] and in the satellite countries (1953-1956), he was obliged to tighten the leading strings around the neck of his subjects. Nonetheless, the living standard in Russia continued to rise, and with it, the *embourgeoisement*.[5]

Unquestionably, too, the people's interest in Communist ideology was declining. In the masses it had probably never gone deeper than protective slogans which gave the mouthers immunity

[4] The latest known occurred on October 3, 1959, in Temir Tao, a steel town in Kazahkstan.

[5] Louis Fischer, in *Russia, America and the World,* argued against the success of this reaction in a well-written paragraph:

"Russians have ever loved their country and hated their government.... Russia has a savage strength, the frustrated power of a giant chained. The nation possesses some uncertain, dark, brooding quality, like a volcano always threatening to vomit forth black lava. The giant can murder and weep, burn and build, worship and scoff, obey and obstruct. Bolsheviks undertook to tame him, gouge out his eyes and cut his tongue and hitch a red cart to him so that he would drag it under the knout. Ivan the Terrible did something similar; Peter the Great likewise.... Lenin was ruthless and maniacally single-tracked. Stalin had steel nerves, no heart and a monster's brain. He transformed the cart into a caterpillar tractor and drove it over fields of living flesh. They buried his mummy in marble by the side of holy Lenin, then called him a butcher and blunderer, yet kept his remains in the mausoleum from the top of which they review the marching millions. Lenin-idolized and Stalin-reviled form the base from which they now rule. Now they have discovered that the giant has kept part of his sight and can mumble and think. He will work when whipped and work when rewarded. The age of the jet and the age of the knout are in conflict. Power without people is an anachronism, an impossibility. So Khrushchev has flung open the gates of the Kremlin in a symbolic gesture and stepped down from its parapets into the streets to talk a lot and listen a little."

from persecution. To be sure, Isaac Deutscher, the Polish ex-Communist, announced that "pure Marxism freed of the orthodox and the ritual" had entered into "the very core of the national consciousness." "Russia," he wrote, was "again pregnant with new world-shaking thoughts and ideas." In a decade it would be a great and prosperous socialist society free from the vulgarities and degradations that had accompanied high standards in capitalist countries. The Soviet peoples, he insisted, were "ready to defend their social system." [6]

Other foreigners of long experience found the Soviet population increasingly apathetic, with a growing resentment and lack of discipline which increased with each loosening of the tyranny.

All in all, grounds for optimism in the eyes of many outsiders. But how much chance was there of its going to the point where the Soviet bosses, of themselves or willy-nilly, would cease their efforts to Communize the world? Would they themselves seek, or be compelled by pressures from below, to remove the barb from "peaceful coexistence" and act "normally"? In other words, how well founded were the hopes that had sustained the "non-provocative" policy of F. D. R., Truman and Eisenhower? Red China had obviously been pushed deep into robotry by the ruling fanatics. Whatever hope of relaxing tensions existed lay in the trend of Soviet society, both the leaders and the mass. How well grounded was such a hope? In short: *was the U.S.S.R. under Khrushchev less a world menace than under Stalin?*

For against the optimistic view acquired by many foreigners in the course of Russian visits and such contacts as a non-Communist foreigner can have with Soviet Communists was the ominous first-hand description of Joseph Novak, a Russian-speaking for-

[6] See Deutscher's *The Great Contest.* But during World War Two, almost a million Russian prisoners of the Nazis fought against Stalin and more might have done so had not Stalin temporarily dropped Communism and appealed to them to defend their "fatherland."

mer Communist who spent a long time in Russia as a young member of the Communist elite.[7] He reported a deeply "brain-washed" society. Its members did not so much acquiesce in Communist ideology and practice as seem unable to imagine anything else. If Novak was right, "thought reform" was the most significant achievement of the Communist Party in forty-three years. Founders like Lenin had consistently sought the *reformation* of society by the *deformation* of the individual. They realized that to succeed in perpetuating party rule in the "new society" they must produce a "Soviet man." This was a human being who no longer needed to be coerced because, thanks to "conditioning," the thought of rebellion or dissent no longer occurred to him. Living under unceasing observation he, like an ant or bee, submitted instinctively to the will and opinion of the hill or hive.[8]

It was thanks to this remarkable achievement, Novak reported, that Khrushchev and his fellow bosses had been able to call off the political police and entrust the enforcement of Communist conformity primarily to the party-controlled group. Pavlov had triumphed. How this worked was described by a visitor returning in 1960 from Communist Czechoslovakia: [9]

"My brother replied, 'No one was forced to take part in the (May Day) parade and the [labor] brigade work is strictly voluntary. . . . But in practice those who fail to join the collective are banned from it and become outcasts from society. The National Committee are obliged to know the daily life of every citizen to the last detail. . . . Each foreman must know whether his employees attend party-convoked meetings and what contribu-

[7] See his *The Future Is Ours, Comrade.*

[8] Lest I seem to exaggerate, see the revised *Soviet System of Government* by John Hazard, *Thought Reform and the Psychology of Totalism* by Robert Jay Lipton. On the other hand one specialist writes me, "There is a wealth of evidence to dispute the thesis that members of Soviet society are ants or bees."

[9] *Features and News from Behind the Iron Curtain,* Vol. XII, No. 27, July 6, 1960.

tions they make there. Every teacher must know not only what his pupils' interests are, but also those of their parents and relatives; how they spend their free time, where they go and whom they visit. If anyone applies for a job, for a flat or for any other personal amenity, he is obliged to state his personal record. Students . . . are judged by . . . their origin, their father's, their mother's and grandparents' past and present professions. It is also important to know . . . their pictures, sculptures, books and periodicals. . . . Habits are a clue as to whether a person's financial means are restricted to official earnings, or whether there may be a suspicion of money from illegal sources. Participation in political gatherings, voluntary brigades, displays of flags in windows —all this is known to the local street committees. Not infrequently mere passivity leads to expulsion from a collective. The culprit loses his job, his flat; he cannot be employed locally and has no other choice than to seek manual badly paid work in localities where there is a shortage of labor, in the border territories, mines, etc. In these circumstances there is no need to proclaim anything as compulsory. Citizens are seldom punished—they are merely educated." [10]

"Thought reform" and the elimination of individual and private aspirations allowed the Party to permit distinguished Soviet specialists, even non-party members, to associate and discuss professional problems with foreign non-Communist colleagues, without fearing serious departure from orthodoxy. Such meetings led unsuspicious foreigners to underestimate the intensity and permanence of Soviet aims.

In short, the thaw in the Soviet Union, *far from marking any defeat of Communism, was a sign of its success.* Brainwashing and de-individualization had been so successful that terror was no longer necessary. Provided they kept up conditioning and limited foreign contacts, the party hierarchy could, it felt, be sure

[10] See also *Soviet Leaders and Mastery over Man,* by Hadley Cantril.

that the Soviet masses would remain a docile instrument for peace or war, for temporary coexistence or a new drive for world rule. If a war was required, the party could always interpret it as defense of the Russian motherland. Moreover, Novak reported *among the Soviet military an almost terrifying acceptance of nuclear conflict.*

Some Western specialists disagreed almost violently. They saw what they felt were sure signs of a basic change, if not in the masses, certainly in the attitude of the leaders who counted. After all, power corrupts and wealth softens even the most dedicated idealogues. What justification was there for this feeling? To answer, one had to analyze the nature of Communism.

Communism started as a utopian dream of anarchy (the state was to "wither away"). What united Communists everywhere was the goal of a world *completely unlike* any previous society. This world required the creation of a group consciousness stronger than any inborn sense of individuality. To achieve such a society, Marx created the myth of its inevitability and spun out an ideology—dialectical materialism—to support the new way of life. Lenin contributed something else—a plan for aiding history by the conscious and unceasing efforts of unswerving revolutionaries.[11]

The first requirement of the revolutionary was the repudiation of all past ("feudal" or "bourgeois") values—an *Umwertung aller Werte* far more radical and brutal than anything dreamed of by Friedrich Nietzsche. For in the coming world, society (and for a long time, the state) was to be everything; the individual a willing social cell.

This most ambitious (and repugnant) of all human endeavors

[11] See Bakunin and Nechaev, *Catechism of a Revolutionist:* "The revolutionist has no personal interests, no affairs, sentiments, attachments, property, not even a name of his own. Everything in him is absorbed by one exclusive interest—the revolution."

required the use of all available means—organization, conspiracy, propaganda and physical force—on a scale never before reached. For since unreformed bourgeois looked upon this "utopia" as indistinguishable from the worst form of tyranny, and considered its ethics monstrous, Communists must prepare to beat down their undying resistance. Since there was a deep and unbridgeable chasm between traditional humanity and the new Communist man, Communism's victory had to be earth-embracing to endure.

That was why Communists required of their subjects not merely compliance, but permanently conditioned acceptance, and sought to bring it about by fear, indoctrination, self-criticism, public confession and unceasing supervision.

The center of the worldwide organization was the party, with branches wherever feasible. This hierarchically organized, iron-disciplined body ruled where possible, conspired where permitted, and under various disguises infiltrated non-Communist bodies in every country. Never before had any group of human beings, united by a common doctrine and a common purpose, given so much time and effort to making and organizing converts. In so doing, their chief instrument was unremitting propaganda in all conceivable forms.

Propaganda in Communist hands assumed techniques and proportions hitherto unknown. In 1959, Suzanne Labin reported, Communism was spending for political warfare all over the globe a *billion* dollars annually and one and a half billion dollars a year indirectly. It maintained literally tens of thousands of agents in countries like France and Italy.

Another propaganda gambit was the appeal to nationalism. Millions of persons who provided the military and economic power that enabled Communism to survive and prosper supposed that they were supporting Russia or China or Cuba. Actually, they were supporting Khrushchev, Mao and Castro and the worldwide totalitarian *apparat*. Moreover, pretended devotion to nationalism enabled Communism to support liberated colonies against their former masters until they too could be brought into the fold. This was imperialism. But the imperialism of the U.S.S.R. was not that of czarist Russia.[12]

What kind of a "nation" was it that could count upon the blind support of "citizens" of ninety other countries? The Communist aim was not a new Russia or a new China but a new world. Therefore, while the West permitted, even urged, new weak countries to remain nonaligned in the worldwide struggle, Moscow and Peiping willingly relinquished not one inch of territory or one individual once they laid hands on them.

In its unceasing efforts to expand, Communism became all things to all men. To those millions of poor everywhere who wanted justice and freedom, economic equality and national independence, it pointed to Marx, to its own collective economy, and to its support of independence movements everywhere outside Communist territory. It promised land reform and full employment. It neglected to emphasize that in the language of the party, democracy meant totalitarian rule, personal freedom equaled complete subjection, peaceful coexistence became the Cold War, truth was any lie that served the immediate purpose of the Communist, and that land reform was speedily followed by collectivization. Nations outside Russia that went Communist retained only nominal independence and were in fact subject to the international party. This did not prevent Khrushchev from appealing to the Russian people with the promise to out-produce America or Mao from telling the Chinese they would finally be in a position to spit in the eye of the hated "foreign devils."

To people who were temperamentally ready to submit to a time or a master, the party insisted on the historical inevita-

[12] For confirmation, see the speech of Allen Dulles, director of the Central Intelligence Agency, August 22, 1960.

bility of its triumph. Why not get on the band wagon in time?

Yet its most successful appeal was to the ambition of energetic, frustrated individuals to whom it offered an unrivaled opportunity for naked rule. For, as practiced by Lenin and his disciples both domestic and foreign, the essence of Communism was power.[13] The bosses talked ethics and economics, adored technology and practiced power politics unremittingly. Doubtless, they rationalized their power drive in the name of a better life for mankind (sometime). But meanwhile they maintained themselves as the *beati possidentes* described by Milovan Djilas, the New Class of the alleged "classless society." By 1961, it was impossible to tell whether the Communist bosses sought power for themselves in order to create a new society or sought a new society in order to keep and extend their personal power.

Meanwhile, the party, the international organization, the power conspiracy, stood with one foot on ideology and the other on Communized national states. Both were essential to its success. Without a common ideology, the peoples would be nations like others with no common international goal. Without control of the military and economic resources of Communized countries, Communist bigwigs would be nothing but the conspirators Lenin and his pals had been before 1917. Only as a worldwide organization with a common ideology masking a common will to power, and with a billion subjects at their disposal, could they wage permanent war, hot or cold, on capitalist society and aspire to world rule. Their successes provided a basis for Khrushchev's claim that the Soviet State would renounce Communism only when "shrimp learn to whistle."

For the West to count on world Communism's abandonment of its virulence or its ultimate aim just when it was massing its

[13] See Sidney Hook, "Political Pretenders and How to Tell Them," *Saturday Review*, December 31, 1960, and Louis Fischer, *idem:* "To the Kremlin mind, power is a substitute for truth."

forces for a new assault was to gamble on a miracle. In fact, although Khrushchev and Mao "reinterpreted" and even "revised" the sacred doctrine as readily as they expunged the names of disgraced former heroes from the history books, they could not do without it and had no intention of trying.[14] Far from relaxing into a traditional pattern, Communist society, especially in Red China, might more and more resemble "Airstrip One" in George Orwell's *1984.*

Many people in the West and the independent East, reluctant to admit this, argued that sooner or later nationalism would prevail. The burden of proof was on them. Perhaps uncertainty sparked the rising tendency of others to base their hope of avoiding a showdown with Communism on something else—the anticipation of rift between the U.S.S.R. and Red China.

Stalin had always scorned the Chinese. In his eyes, the U.S.S.R. was to remain the citadel and headquarters of the spreading Communist empire. The Chinese were all right in their place—a secondary place. Yet from the moment Mao had seized China, he entered into a sort of rivalry with Stalin, refusing to submit to his dictation. Khrushchev was more accommodating, particularly after the warning he and Bulganin got from Mao during their visit to Peiping in 1954. Nikita made a whole series of "concessions," territorial and other, to his Far Eastern ally. Nonetheless, from 1958 on, he and Mao engaged in a public dispute concerning the proper method for extending the revolution.

Topics of difference were, first, whether Communism could conquer the planet without a war—Khrushchev saying it could; second, whether an undeveloped country like China could "leap forward" into Communism—Mao affirming; and third, whether Communism gained by supporting bourgeois governments in new countries—Mao dissenting.

[14] See Khrushchev's Report of the Moscow Conference of the Communist Parties, December, 1960.

In many other respects the two countries differed. The Chinese were an unusually proud people with an ineradicable superiority complex. For the first time in a century, Communism freed them from the pressures of "foreign devils." [15] Moreover, like the Yugoslavs, the Chinese Communists had taken power with only indirect Soviet help. Another difference: though larger than the United States, Red China was oppressively overcrowded and pitifully poor while the still larger U.S.S.R. remained relatively empty and prosperous. Red Russia was a heavily industrialized country, one of the two major powers in the world conflict. Red China, because of the density of its population, remained the most vulnerable of all countries to nuclear warfare. Relatively to the Big Two, its military power would continue to decline until it had nuclear weapons.[16] Nonetheless, Mao, an egomaniac to begin with and a disciple of Stalin, considered himself far closer to Lenin than any other living Communist, and the equal, rather than the satellite, of Khrushchev.

To prove his superior wisdom, Mao ignored Moscow's warnings about haste and, after an experiment with leniency (the program poetically named "let a hundred flowers bloom") which revealed lasting widespread hostility to his regime, he herded much of his unhappy population into "people's communes." These were human hives in which both town and country people, deprived of freedom and the most elementary comfort, overworked, underfed and brain-washed into mental vacuity, toiled to make Red China a great industrial country. None could be sure that Mao's subsequent relaxation of the drive for communes was permanent.

These differences left plenty of room for disagreement between Khrushchev and Mao. In consequence, many of the same West-

[15] Joseph Levinson, *Liang Ch'i-ch'ao and the Mind of Modern China,* insisted that the Chinese had "adopted communism in order to achieve superiority."

[16] Stefan T. Possony: *Strategy* in *Bear and Dragon.*

erners who had first dreamed of detaching Red China from Red Russia now salvaged their failing hope by turning it upside down. Skillful Western diplomacy, they argued, could detach the U.S.S.R. from Red China. The chief author of this reversal was a German physician, Wilhelm Starlinger. In 1954, after five years of imprisonment in Russia, he returned to Germany to write a book, *Die Grenzen der Sovietmacht.* He argued "biologically" that overpopulation would ultimately drive the Chinese over their borders into Soviet Manchuria, Mongolia and other regions. Fearful of China's numbers and growing power, the Kremlin would, Starlinger assumed, seek the support of the West. Communism, divided, would no longer be a world menace.

This thesis interested Chancellor Adenauer of Germany, who managed to communicate his interest to President de Gaulle of France. French politician Paul Reynaud, after a visit to Red China, predicted that the nation's nationalism would turn into Pan-Asian frenzy. Peiping would seek to "redeem" all the Asian subjects of the U.S.S.R.—the Kazaks, Kirghiz, Uzbeks and Turkomans of Central Asia; the Tunguses, Buryats and Yakuts of Siberia; and perhaps even the Bashkirs, Kalmuks and Tatars of Russia proper. Here lay the root of a coming row.

Britain's brash Sovietologist, Edward Crankshaw, threw caution to the winds and announced that "either the Russians start trying to woo the Chinese by returning to Stalin's ways or else the rift becomes a gulf and the Chinese, without a restraining hand, begin to run wild." Edvard Kardely, Yugoslav's chief Marxist priest, decided that China "needed a war."

Other Westerners, like Starlinger, maintained that Khrushchev so feared that the Chinese would drag him into a nuclear struggle over Formosa or India that he was looking for a chance to "disentangle" the U.S.S.R. from an alliance it no longer completely controlled.

Against this argument stood, however, the brute fact that Khrushchev, having watched Stalin alienate Yugoslavia by his bullying, seemed in no hurry to repeat the experiment with China.

To ease Mao's position and keep up the flow of machines to Peiping, he reversed, in 1955, Malenkov's popular emphasis on more consumer goods for Russians and threw Malenkov out. And in December, 1960, just when certain Western mouths were watering at the prospect of an open rift between the Bear and the Tiger, the two came to at least nominal agreement at the meeting of the International Communist Parties in Moscow—and together snarled at capitalism.[17]

The vital question was not, of course, whether Nikita and Mao saw eye to eye on all problems—they obviously did not—but whether their differences were any greater or more significant than those of, say, Dulles and Eden at the time of Suez, or of Macmillan and Adenauer on the European Common Market, or of De Gaulle and Eisenhower on France's need for nuclear weapons.

Many of the best authorities thought they were not.[18] They cited impressive evidence: numerous references by leading Chinese to the "lasting, invincible and unswerving" unity of the Chinese and Russian peoples (Mao's expression), and to the "great leap forward" as "inseparably connected with assistance from the Soviet Union and other fraternal countries." In 1957, the Chinese Ambassador in Moscow rhapsodized that "the friendship between the Chinese and Soviet peoples is higher than the sky, deeper than the sea . . . like a pine in the forest, always fresh, never dropping."

Moreover, Red China was establishing ever more industries in

[17] Somewhat later (Washington *Post*, Feb. 11, 1960), Crankshaw claimed to have read "a fully documented report of the charges and counter charges between Peking and Moscow at the Moscow conference." To him it confirmed "the strained state of Chinese-Soviet relations."

[18] Among others: David Nelson Rowe, Karl Wittfogel, Paul Linebarger, Philip Mosely, Boris Souvarine, Branko Lazitch and Suzanne Labin.

Manchuria, a Soviet trap in case of war between the two countries, while Russia steadily built up new factories along the Chinese border. Soviet production quotas continued to include aid for China. Eighty-five per cent of China's foreign trade in 1959 was with Russia.[19] In the heat of the 1959 "controversy," Khrushchev promised Mao a loan of one and a quarter billion dollars for more equipment and planned to build sixty new enterprises for him. The U.S.S.R. had already given China at least 750 million dollars in military equipment, had supplied nuclear research reactors, short-range missiles with the warheads in charge of Russian assistants and at least two thousand warplanes; was furnishing fifty per cent of the country's oil needs and a good deal of steel, as well as thousands and thousands of technicians—some of whom suddenly went home or were recalled. In fact, the Soviets were the chief creators of China's power and could throttle down growth at will. Were these the acts of a frightened or angry country toward its neighbor? More important, the four-thousand-mile common border was lightly guarded.

Moreover, every foreign strategist knew that to continue expanding, by whatever means, each country needed the other. Neither was producing enough food, despite the claims of Communist bureaucrats who considered statistics "weapons in the class struggle."

Some Western experts went further. They charged Moscow and Peiping with deliberately deceiving the West with stories of pretended quarrels. Their differences were on matters that united them. Neither could yet afford to "make peace or wage atomic war." "Separation from Russia" helped China "best to carry out military aggression without reprisal," according to David Nelson

[19] See *Is There a Sino-Soviet Split?* by Suzanne Labin and Christopher Emmet, Orbis, Spring, 1960. Other experts claimed that trade with the whole Communist bloc was only two-thirds of the Chinese total. It should be noted that all Red Chinese statistics were liable to be doctored while the U.S.S.R. measured production in rubles of uncertain or arbitrary value.

Rowe. Thus while one was engaged in grab, the other was tut-tutting and sweet-talking to prevent serious Western counter-action.[20] Had the quarrels been serious, both countries would have done their best to conceal them.

While a future struggle between two Communist states was not excluded, it was far less likely to occur while both were progress-ing successfully toward a common goal than when, having reached that goal, they started to divide the spoils, or when, having been thwarted in their common ambition, each put the blame upon the other. For, to quote Karl A. Wittfogel, only victims of illusion would expect Mao, or whoever succeeded him, to desert what the Chinese, like the Soviet leaders, hoped would be the "bandwagon of an historically unavoidable global victory." Current differences were presumably of degree and timing, not of basic purpose. In fact, squabbles over the best method of furthering the revolution reminded one of the two cannibals who had caught a plump missionary. One advocated killing him outright by a blow on the neck, the other preferred breaking his bones gently and leaving him to expire in the nearby river, thoroughly tenderized.

By 1961 many former optimists had to concede that Commu-nism remained "planetary imperialism." Far from relaxing the Cold War, Khrushchev and Mao were stepping it up at times and places of their own choosing. The means shifted, the end re-mained the same.[21] On several occasions, Philip Mosely noted in *The Kremlin and World Politics,* Communist leaders revealed their belief in their ability to "force a new crisis close to the brink

[20] Labin and Emmet wrote: "It was the Chinese military tactician Sun Tse who in the Sixth Century, B.C., advised those who wanted to expand their territories to lull the vigilance of the nations they coveted by dissemi-nating rumors of internal dissension in their own countries."

[21] See Elliott Goodman, *The Soviet Design for a World State,* p. 472: "The conscious and outward thrust of Soviet power maintains as its objective the absorption of all the nations of the world into the Soviet body politic and ultimately the reshaping of their patterns of life into the single all-embracing mold of a Soviet world state."

of war and to compel the other side to flinch from this fateful decision." Those Westerners reluctant to credit so enormous an ambition needed only to plow through the dreary but alarming reports on the Communist Parties Moscow Conference of November-December, 1960.

In the middle of the Fifties, Red Russia and Red China divided the non-Communist areas into spheres of influence, with a third sphere, formerly that of the French comrades, for the Italian Communist Party.

They also appeared to have divided the roles. Khrushchev's undertaking was to establish friendly relations with the American President and prevent any consolidation of Western alliances [22] or any increase in military expenditures. He also planned to paralyze the activities of the United Nations until he got it made over to suit his purpose and obtained the admission of Red China as a member. This last, by discrediting Formosa, would pave the way for Mao's peaceful conquest of that island and perhaps drive Japan, South Korea and the Philippines into non-alignment.

Mao's job meanwhile was to soften up the rickety Southeast Asian states preparatory to taking them over. Past success seemed to have convinced both Communist leaders that they could, with time and unceasing effort, outdistance "decadent" America.

No wonder that David Nelson Rowe urged the United States unequivocally to adopt a strategy for *unlimited war that would include Communist China.*

[22] Nikita Khrushchev to the Moscow Congress: "The window of the so-called Atlantic solidarity hides an ugly picture of internal discords and conflicts; the opposition to U. S. leadership and dictates is increasing."

Chapter XI

THE BALANCE OF TERROR

"The fear of death, the desire to survive at any cost or price in human degradation, has been the greatest ally of tyranny, past or present."

—SIDNEY HOOK

Between the late Forties, when the A-bombs began to roll in, and the late Fifties, when the U.S.S.R. added H-bombs to superior rockets, the United States had an impressive military superiority over its chief adversary. During the first part of this period Washington could have liberated the captive peoples of Europe either by an ultimatum or with small losses.

The situation began to change in 1949, with the Soviet's first atomic explosion, four years after the United States'. It changed again in 1953, when Moscow staged a thermonuclear explosion only a few months after America. In 1957, the Soviet Sputnik warned that for the first time in its history the United States was fully open to an armed attack, further, one of almost unimaginably destructive power.[1]

[1] In 1945, Dr. Vannevar Bush, wartime director of the Office of Scientific Research and Development, considered the construction of an accurate rocket impossible, and his decision played a large part in the temporary abandonment of the effort in the United States.

Until 1953, thanks to a superior Air Force, an American policy of "massive retaliation" was feasible. After that date the U.S.S.R. was well on the way to making "massive retaliation," even against faraway America, a two-way street. In other words, as former Secretary of State Dean Acheson insisted in *American Strategy for the Nuclear Age,* "We waited until the Soviet Union possessed nuclear weapons and then announced the doctrine of complete reliance on them." After 1957, "massive retaliation" simply faded out of American thinking, although official United States policy never acknowledged that fact.

Never had a major power balance shifted so swiftly. At the end of World War Two, it would have seemed incredible that the United States could lose its technological superiority—and to such a competitor. But there was the unhappy fact. Neither Britain's creation of a small nuclear supporting force nor Eisenhower's nonchalance could alter it.

Even worse, the "equalization" in nuclear weapons and delivery systems left the Soviets ahead in almost all those other weapons which U. S. planners, concentrating on planes with big bombs, had considered unnecessary.

Nonetheless, the President decided that a "balance" of military power in major weapons between the U.S.A. and the U.S.S.R. was the cheapest and safest course. Real superiority on *either* side, he reasoned, could jeopardize the peace or, at the least, unleash a costly arms race, which was the last thing he wanted because he considered it unnecessary. Historically minded Americans might observe that twice in their own lifetime—in 1914 and in 1939—reliance on such uncertain "balances of power" had led to general war, while the longest peaces recorded had rested, respectively, upon the overwhelming military preponderance of imperial Rome and imperial Britain. Dean Acheson might protest that "one does not become stronger by becoming weaker." No matter. The President and, later, Secretary Herter, were willing to settle for "security without surrender," and meanwhile do everything possible to persuade Communism to call off, or limit, the armaments race on satisfactory terms.

For General Eisenhower had decided war was "unthinkable" and in his "peace crusade" he had the wholehearted support, at least theoretically, of most human beings.

Unfortunately, the end of the Second World War coincided with an open bid for world empire by men in whose eyes human beings were expendable. Lenin had stated that a war was to be evaluated "not by the number of its casualties but by its political consequences." Mao Tse-tung boasted that with the death of half its population—say, three hundred million people—Red China would be a better place. Even after 1956, when Khrushchev elevated the old Communist routine of "peaceful coexistence" to a major propaganda weapon, he still insisted that any "war of liberation waged by Communism was by definition defensive and justified." Communist leaders continually warned their peoples to expect protracted conflict.

How then could the "peace-loving" peoples be sure that Moscow and Peking would not resort to war to extend Communism whenever and by whatever means this could be done cheaply enough? Was not the Soviet Union's endless talk of disarmament and peace intended to tranquilize its victims until it grew large enough to swallow them?

By the late Fifties, the United States and the U.S.S.R. found themselves in a historically unique situation. Like two scorpions, each country claimed the ability to kill the other. The scorpion first stung could, with luck, strike back and kill the aggressor. It was, as Anastas Mikoyan now observed, no longer certain who was encircling whom.

In another way, the two powers resembled rival Indian tribes. A raiding party that destroyed the adversary's camp by a sneak attack found that its own camp had subsequently been burned by the other's raiding party.

Or one could compare them to two termite warriors facing each other, each formidable above the waist but defenseless below, hence unable to turn and run. So long as the U.S.S.R. and the U.S.A. both maintained enough power to honor their unwritten "suicide pact," they could, they hoped, count on preserving the peace. For it seemed a reasonable assumption that no modern leader would either embark upon a war from which his own country would emerge a battered and depopulated wreck or provoke lesser conflicts that might become general. Such, at least, were the current theories.

In consequence, many Westerners believed peace was more secure than before the invention of nuclear bombs. Britain's Defense Minister, Harold Watkinson, became lyrical in praise of the stalemate. "If we do away with nuclear weapons," he argued, "we open the way once again to war as an instrument in the hands of ruthless aggressors.... Can we say that the threat of mutual nuclear annihilation is an unmitigated moral evil if it saves us from horrors of this magnitude?"

Admiral Arleigh Burke, Chairman of the Joint Chiefs of Staff, rejoiced that "we need only what it takes to wreak sufficient damage upon the enemy to make it unprofitable for him to initiate an all-out nuclear attack."

What "it took" was nuclear forces at a minimum level. Eventually the U.S.S.R. would lose its imperialistic ambition, or fall out with more belligerent Red China, or "something."

Actually, the situation was anything but reassuring to many persons. American and allied planners might examine and reexamine the situation, government experts might express their relative reassurance, but they did not make the "balance of terror" entirely acceptable, for several reasons.

Most important, the balance was manifestly asymmetrical. The

United States, save under intolerable provocation or without a direct Soviet attack on a major ally, would not strike first. The President had made this clear, U.S. generals and admirals repeated it as a matter of course, U.S. strategical studies took it for granted.

On the other hand, no American could be sure that the U.S.S.R. would not attack the United States at the first opportunity that assured it relative impunity. Soviet Marshal Rodion Malinovsky might talk "defense" and concentrate his threats on "inevitable retaliation" against the "capitalist imperialist" camp. But no American could know exactly just how much of Red Russia an American retaliatory force must be able to demolish, how many tens of millions of Soviet subjects it must be able to kill by blast, fire and fall-out, in order to deter a Communist first strike. Back in Stalin's time, August 20, 1950, Radio Moscow had served notice that all "those acts are moral that contribute to the building of Communist society."

The balance was asymmetrical in yet another way. Officers like General Maxwell Taylor and Admiral Burke repeatedly cautioned the United States against preparing an "overkill"—producing an unnecessary number of H-bombs, missile-carrying nuclear submarines, and relatively invulnerable solid-fuel intercontinental ballistic missiles. They insisted that the price of unneeded weapons could better be spent on smaller forces usefully in forestalling and suppressing local acts of Communist arson. The United States had not seriously gone about acquiring all available *defense*—anti-missile missiles and shelters for civilians, to name a few—*and felt it should not do so*. In fact, Jerome B. Wiesner, a nuclear physicist and later a high scientific adviser to President Kennedy, warned that the "missile deterrence system" would be "unbalanced by the development of a highly effective anti-missile system."

Yet Soviet leaders continued to "concentrate on the military sector of their economy." They not only poured out Sputniks instead of fin-tailed cars, they also devoted huge sums to the armed forces and to weapons of all types. There was reason to believe that they had started a civilian-defense program that included the possible quick evacuation of their cities, either as a prelude to a first strike or as a decisive weapon in political warfare.

For, unlike the American Administration, Soviet leaders did *not* expect to win a third world war by a blitz or within three weeks. All their planning and their preparations indicated that they considered themselves involved in a protracted conflict in which war, if it came, might last for many years. Therefore, they prepared graduated forces for both offensive and defensive—everything from H-bombs and ICBM's to specially trained guerrillas, "volunteers" and disguised saboteurs and political agents. It was as though they had equipped their scorpion with not one lethal stinger but a dozen graduated sorts. In the face of such an arsenal, finite deterrence (no "overkill") had little or nothing to say.

Finite deterrence also looked unreliable for psychological reasons. Westerners who said they preferred Communism to risking nuclear war ("better Red than dead") might become a majority if the danger became overwhelming. Democratic leaders could not ignore their people's fears, whereas Khrushchev and Mao enjoyed almost total authority. At some point a U.S. Administration could decide that the defense of, say, little Denmark, was not worth the death of fifty million Americans. Even the barest suspicion that Washington had so concluded could be an open invitation to Communist leaders to take over that country by that graduated blackmail for which they had long prepared themselves.

A future American Administration, concentrating exclusively on nuclear weapons, might decide that since overseas allies no longer added much of anything to American military strength, it would do well to divest themselves of them, even if they were certain to drift into the Communist camp.

A Communist bloc of a billion and a half people, including West Europe, could outstrip the United States in the scientific, technological and military fields, assume gradual control over all non-aligned and undeveloped areas of the earth, and eventually bring America to terms without fighting.

The balance of terror was, moreover, no stronger than human prudence. How firm was that foundation? In the absence of full knowledge of what the Soviets were doing (especially after the canceling of U-2 flights) American planners depended upon what they liked to call a "calculated risk." But a calculated risk could turn out to be a risk that was incalculable. Should, for instance, the United States base the size of its armament on its *estimate* of what the Soviets were producing, or on its *knowledge* of what they were *able* to produce?

Still again, how judge what was going on in those Marxist-marred minds in the Kremlin? How be sure that at some point the wily Mr. K., for all his bonhomie, might not decide that further peaceful coexistence was too dangerous? Could not a situation arise in the Communist world—say the threat of popular insurrection or a menacing split between the two Red giants—in which the Kremlin would decide that the risk of attacking the United States was less than that of letting matters take an anti-Communist course elsewhere?

If the United States discovered that through excessive economy it was lagging in the arms race, how long would its moral inhibition against launching a first strike hold? Suppose that the President suddenly learned that the Soviets were planning an early attack. A faulty estimate of the intentions of a ruthless enemy could pave the way to nuclear hell.

Many, though by no means all, Western experts felt that the apparently inevitable spread of nuclear weapons to other countries would increase the danger of either accidental or "catalytic" war.

And of course any small war could, as the Kremlin repeatedly warned, turn into a general holocaust.

These risks were all inherent in the current situation. But there was worse. The deepest students of the problem were realizing that the current stalemate was unstable.[2] Either effective unilateral defense measures by one side or the discovery of a new weapon that could be temporarily kept secret (Byzantium survived for centuries by keeping secret the formula of Greek fire) and used before it could be imitated, might change everything.[3] *The side that established an unshakable monopoly of outer space, if this turned out to be possible, could perhaps achieve world rule without the need for fighting.*

A former member of the Atomic Energy Commission, Thomas E. Murray, warned that the Soviets might be well on the way to producing an "N-bomb"—a device without blast or fall-out that destroyed all life within its explosive range. Moreover, if Soviet scientists discovered a safer means of adopting one of the chemical weapons that comprised one-sixth of their entire stock of arms, the Kremlin might yield to the temptation to use it.

Obviously, the side that first built a defense even fifty per cent efficient would possess a crucial advantage and enjoy a freedom of political action forbidden to the defenseless. Many of the elements of such defense already existed and others were in prospect. The production of a phenomenally successful anti-missile missile would completely change the political picture. Or the U.S.S.R. might find an easy way to detect and destroy the Polaris-carrying nuclear submarines upon whose invulnerability the

[2] Such as Herman Kahn, *On Nuclear War.*

[3] For a remarkable description of the research and development plans of the U.S. Army, see Lieut. General Arthur G. Trudeau, *Congressional Record,* July 5, 1960, p. A5843.

United States was relying as deterrent, or find a way of shooting down its missiles. In fact, as matters stood, effective defense rather than further offense was most likely to upset the balance of terror.

Even earlier (June, 1959) a report of hearings before the Congressional Joint Committee on Atomic Energy contained a sinister passage: "Recent calculations tend to cast doubt on the widely held notion that nuclear weapons have created a balance of terror."

In 1960, at Department of Defense appropriation hearings, the following occurred:

CONGRESSMAN MAHON: In this arms race . . . the Soviet Union has been closing the gap very markedly. Would you agree?

SECRETARY OF DEFENSE MCELROY: Yes.

MAHON: Our position has been deteriorating since World War Two, relatively speaking?

MCELROY: Only relatively speaking. . . .

MAHON: Of course we have been getting stronger but they have been getting stronger faster.

MCELROY: That is correct.

MAHON: How long is this trend going to continue?

MCELROY: It cannot continue to the point where this country is unable to protect its national security.

But perhaps it could. The fear of this lay behind the altercation over the American missile gap predicted by some for the period between 1961 and 1965. The United States initial striking force—airplanes plus missiles—might still be preponderant. But if the country jogged along at the Eisenhower gait of production while the Kremlin produced all the missiles it could, the U.S.S.R. might surpass the United States.

Perhaps it had already done so. The U.S. Air Force, always impatient of any defense establishment incapable of an irresistible "first strike," suddenly leaked an extraordinary story to the press. It appeared in the *Washington Star,* December 19, 1960.

Suppose, the Air Force speculated, that in 1963 the Soviets launch an all-out attack upon the United States. "Explosions incinerate bomber bases and missile launching sites from one end of the United States to the other. Few Soviet missiles miss their targets."

What is left of the U.S. striking force strikes back at Soviet cities. Yet Soviet forces attack the remaining American bases a second time. Then having destroyed America's offensive and defensive capacity, Soviet-manned bombers kill off American cities one by one. When it is over, one hundred and eighty million of one hundred and ninety million Americans are dead. The Soviets have fifty million dead. So concluded the Air Force's electronic computers.

Or suppose, on the same day, that in retaliation for a conventional Soviet attack on West Germany, Americans strike first. They destroy a number of Soviet cities and bases. What is left of the Soviet forces strikes back at American cities. Whereupon American forces launch a second attack. Still the United States suffers more—one hundred and ten million dead against "only" seventy-five million Russians.

But a different test: instead of including Soviet cities in its targets, the U.S. striking force limits its first attack to previously located bomber fields, missile sites, nuclear submarine pens and control centers in the U.S.S.R. The Soviet remainder strikes back at American military targets only. Surviving American forces—all but a few—attack strategic targets a second time and finish them off. The Soviets have now exhausted their punch, the United States has not. The Soviets surrender. Total human losses on both sides: three million Americans, five million Russians. This is less than the losses of the two world wars.

Repeating its calculations, the Air Force found that no matter what assumptions it made, the more the United States concentrated on purely military targets, ignoring Soviet cities, the smaller its human losses and the greater its chance of winning.

This apocalyptic statement by the Air Force aroused both opposition and irony in the other American forces. The mildest criticism was that its assumption that the U.S.S.R. could be induced to spare American cities did not reflect Soviet military thinking. Yet the conclusion was startling—for whatever reason, exclusive reliance by the United States on mutual deterrence by the threat of mass slaughter could lead to national catastrophe. For in 1961 the balance of terror was a myth.[4] The advantage was on the Soviet side.

Yet at about the same time, a persistent rumor swept the city of Washington to the effect that despite big talk, *neither the U.S.A. nor the U.S.S.R. as yet possessed a single ICBM certain, under wartime conditions, to hit its target.* After all, neither side had been able or willing to carry out adequate testing.

The Cold War was not a stalemate but an open race. Communists thought it might last a century. And Communism had never subjugated a single new country without military intervention or overt military pressure.

Mao Tse-tung had urged all comrades to realize that "political power grows from the barrels of a gun—in fact, the whole world can be remodeled only with the gun."

Saying that war was "unthinkable" conceivably made it more likely than considering it highly probable and drawing the necessary conclusions.[5]

[4] A Republican Party task force flatly denied this: "It is only by exercises of science fiction fantasy that critics can say Russia might destroy our retaliatory power. These writers are not in fact able to say that Russia actually possesses such power. Such criticism characteristically says that Russia could do such and such if Russia had such and such."

[5] For a remarkable study of the situation, see "Strategy for the New Frontier" by Klausewitz Wilhelm Rudolf, in *Army*, January, 1961.

But what conclusions?

Here the donnybrook started in the Western World. A small undaunted group of American planners had a radical answer—they would make the "balance of terror" as "sure as doom!"

If the current model H-bomb could not indefinitely frighten the rival nations into keeping the peace, then they would make bombs that could! A single *begaton* weapon, with a charge equal to a billion tons of TNT, could be built into a Nova rocket and, if exploded in orbit, burn everything within a radius of five hundred miles. If such a monster did not panic Communism into accepting arms control with full inspection, then American scientists could go a step further and produce a *gigaton* bomb that could destroy a continent—or maybe the earth. Faced with the certainty of absolute suicide, if it started a war, the U.S.S.R. would have to come to terms.

This would be deterrence with a vengeance. But even without it, the current "balance of terror" owed much of its efficacy (such as it was) to the fact that it was based on the potential slaughter of tens of millions of civilians and the destruction of whole countries. Yet few experts were yet committed to the full development and, if possible, exclusive use of "cleaner" weapons, which other experts considered both feasible and proper.

Instead, beginning with the explosion of the first A-bomb over Hiroshima in 1945, conscience-stricken American physicists, soon reinforced by foreign colleagues, started arguing that superweapons made peace an immediate necessity. A new war would, they stated, end the human race. Or civilization. Or the two chief adversaries. Or cripple future generations. Here these nuclear pacifists joined the religious pacifists. But with a difference. To religious men, killing was wrong, whether of one or a billion human beings. To the scientists and the professors, teachers and other "men of good will" who joined the nuclear peace crusade, war became "unthinkable" only when the number of casualties reached a certain figure—nobody could say precisely how many millions or tens of millions.

This vagueness did not seriously bother the crusading pacifists. For they were relying for their dynamism not upon accuracy of prediction but upon a curious marriage of fear and reason. Among them all, the most extreme was possibly Karl Jaspers, father (or co-father) of modern existentialism. He boldly proclaimed that to save mankind from destruction, the first step was to "increase the fear . . . of the people . . . to overpowering force" leading "to rational vision rather than blind panic." Reason at the level of "transcendence" could create a New Man.

It *could* because it *must*. For according to a British pacifist, Philip Toynbee, *anything* was better than a policy that allowed for the possibility of nuclear war. To be sure, chemist Harrison Brown, after insisting for years that without nuclear disarmament nuclear war was "certain," eventually reduced the certainty to a probability. But he still affirmed that there could be no winner in an arms race. For in estimating the casualties of such a war, nuclear pacifists regularly took the highest available figure. Scientist-novelist C. P. Snow informed the American Association for the Advancement of Science that it was "quite unrealistic and very dangerous to imagine that the West as a whole can expect a permanent and decisive lead over the East as a whole."

This was quite a statement, but one typical of the nuclear pacifists. Some insisted that *total* disarmament was not enough. Meanwhile, no provocation of the U.S.S.R. A few warned that giving nuclear power to Germany would provoke an immediate Soviet pre-emptive strike at the United States. One Cyril Osborne a Conservative Member of Parliament, returned from Red China to announce that nothing could prevent a world war if the United States did not abandon its support of Chiang Kai-shek on Taiwan. Harrison Brown predicted that as the Russians "got ahead" (why should they?), the United States and its allies were likely to undertake desperate, erratic, unauthorized action.[6] Anyhow, Brown argued, even if the arms race did not spark a nuclear war, a prolonged arms race would drive the peoples of both sides into a nightmare-like cave existence.

However unsubstantiated, such statements spread through Western universities like a flu epidemic. Pundit after pundit took them up without close examination and made them his own. Charles A. Barker, Johns Hopkins historian, wrote to me that "in the future we *must* get on somehow with our fellowmen, the Russians especially, by reason mainly or *we do not survive.*"

Considering that successive American Administrations had, since December, 1941, sought nothing so much as getting on with the Russians on a basis Americans could decently accept, this seemed an irrational approach.

During years of negotiations, the United States had offered in vain no less than nine interdependent proposals for gradual disarmament.[7] Was an agreement on this subject possible with an imperialist power whose major prophet, Nikolai Lenin, had written: "Only after the proletariat has disarmed the bourgeoisie will it be able, without betraying its world historical mission, to throw all armaments on the scrap heap"?

Some experts considered nuclear disarmament impossible.[8] Eugene Rabinowitch, editor of the influential *Bulletin of the Atomic Scientists,* had as early as the end of 1954 written:

"Effectively controlled atomic disarmament has ceased to be possible and all attempts to find a compromise solution are there-

[6] Brown, like Castro's defender, C. Wright Mills, postulated the existence of an "American military elite dedicated to a position of perpetual hostility to the U.S.S.R." Yet he would have cried foul, had someone charged him with belonging to an American academic elite dedicated to the cause of submission to Moscow.

[7] The Box Score (*U. S. News and World Report,* April 25, 1960): "690 meetings, 1,400 hours of talk, 15 million words, still no agreement in sight."

[8] Among them Salvador de Madariaga, Robert R. Bowie, Alistair Buchan, Harold Urey and Edward Teller.

fore bound to remain futile. Mankind will have to live, from now on, with unlimited and unchecked stockpiles of atomic and thermonuclear explosives piling up first in America and the Soviet Union, then in Great Britain and later in other countries as well."

Yet, becoming impatient, he wrote six years later that the situation had improved because "the fear of war has, if anything, increased on both sides."

Nonetheless, whatever their minor differences, nuclear pacifists agreed the United States must somehow end the "balance of terror" and with it the current rush toward "nuclear destruction." A formal agreement to refrain from further nuclear tests might still stop the spread of nuclear weapons to other countries, and lead the rival governments to put an end to the "giant retaliatory systems" by other forms of arms control.

And so far so good. Few Westerners objected to continued efforts at finding out whether any arms control was possible. All normal people hoped that war was on the way out, even though the connection between disarmament and peace was tenuous. At the least, a disarmed China could not try to conquer Formosa or repopulate the fertile and underpopulated lands of Southeast Asia. Yet a China that refused to follow the U.S.S.R. into disarmament would either cause a break or show up the falsity of the Kremlin's offer.

But to change what Norman Cousins called the "context" of the disarmament argument, all nuclear powers had to move at the same time. Hard-boiled and experienced Jules Moch of France, a passionate disarmament negotiator, might believe that suffering in World War Two had made "the Russians" ready to do so. But what about the Kremlin?

Nuclear pacifists brushed aside such questions as carping. For they wanted no weakening of the stalemate of terror until such time as the rival camps came to terms on disarmament.

Consequently, they opposed building civilian shelters, although competent investigators insisted that these could reduce the number of civilian victims of an assumed attack on the United States from at least twenty-five to six per cent. They were cool on evacuation plans, though Sweden had adopted one. They opposed a shift of target strategy away from enemy cities to enemy military centers, which would permit an American striking force to rely primarily upon "cleaner" bombs. They had no enthusiasm for anti-missile missiles. For their overwhelming purpose was, as stated by Karl Jaspers, to frighten the free peoples to the point where they found the prospect of *any war* intolerable.

Obviously, such blind devotion to peace minimized the importance of human freedom and the difficulty of eliminating power politics from a world hopelessly divided into three parts—one committed to the open society, another to totalitarianism, and a third to non-aligned independence.[9]

Basically, the great arms debate of 1961, at least in the West, was between those who sincerely believed they could count on the stalemate of terror to lead to the elimination of war (or at least of nuclear war) and those who remained convinced that peace without freedom was valueless and that, short of change in the Communist countries, the free countries would have to ignore the nuclear risk and rely for survival upon their own unity, strength, determination and technology.

For in all likelihood there existed a third alternative to nuclear war or surrender. With a sufficient effort the West could alter the balance of terror to its own advantage.

A change in strategy somewhat as the Air Force advocated, substituting enemy military targets for enemy cities, and employing only "cleaner" bombs limited to air-bursts (unless the adversary resorted to "dirty" tactics) would lessen the fear that para-

[9] See Robert W. Tucker: "Nuclear Pacifism—Some Reflections on the Community of Fear," *The New Republic,* February 6, 1961.

lyzed the Western peoples. Invulnerable "spy" satellites (predicted for a relatively near future) would leave no nation with the possibility of launching a sneak attack.

The spread of nuclear weapons was a greater danger to the U.S.S.R. than to the United States. For it would multiply the divisions within the Communist bloc and cause the Kremlin continually to modify any conceivable plans for a first nuclear strike.

President Eisenhower and his advisers had overlooked (or found inacceptable) the fact that the United States could support an arms race far better than the U.S.S.R. Such a race, while not driving rich America into bankruptcy, could cause political stresses within the U.S.S.R. To keep up with a United States that doubled its current arms appropriation (and economized by sharing scientific research and technological skills with its major allies), the United States could compel the Soviets to invest in arms *almost forty per cent of their gross national product.*

America had unemployment, vast unused industrial resources and an enormous capacity for growth. It could greatly increase its armaments without restricting consumption. The tightly stretched U.S.S.R. would find any reduction in consumer goods politically dangerous. A reduction in its industrial and machine exports to China would be disastrous.[10]

The West could afford to produce whatever was necessary for its survival. It could, when necessary, build civilian shelters which, even if never used, would reassure its peoples. In addition to large nuclear weapons, it had the means to provide balanced forces—tactical, nuclear and conventional weapons—to meet any emergency. America could officially make plans to meet graduated aggression by graduated deterrence, and stop scaring its allies into panic or non-alignment by stubbornly insisting on

[10] For the outstanding discussion of this and other American advantages, see *A Forward Strategy for America* by Robert Strausz-Hupé, William R. Kintner and Stefan T. Possony.

"massive retaliation" (the "bigger bang for a buck") as the only policy it could afford.

In fact, the mere announcement of a Western determination to achieve preponderance in all necessary categories of weapons would conceivably be decisive in bringing about an agreement on arms control. For in Communist eyes, the U.S.S.R., the powerhouse of world revolution, was far too precious to be risked. So long as the men in the Kremlin faced a vulnerable and undecided America, they need not take its disarmament proposals seriously. Once they found themselves unable to keep level in an armament race, the awful danger and cost of their fanatical campaign to subvert the world would be clear.[11]

Nuclear pacifists objected that such a decision would "inevitably" increase the danger of destroying the human race. But since they held that the existing situation made war "virtually certain" anyway, an American attempt to render itself invulnerable could not increase the peril. A substantial increase in the relative power of the West would fortify both peace and freedom. Certainly it was preferable to sitting still and watching Communism advance, and crying "peace, peace" where there was no peace.

Lenin had warned, "Ultimately, one or the other must conquer."

Almost surely it would be the side with the steadiest nerves, the most flexible strategy, the greatest resources, most balanced forces, and the will to win. For, as Fisher Ames had noted a century earlier, "It is a law of politics as well as of physics that a body in motion must overcome an equal body at rest."

[11] For an argument that the U.S.S.R. could not survive total disarmament, see Norman A. Bailey, *Business Week*, January 28, 1961.

Chapter XII

AN END TO MAKE-BELIEVE

"We have known what is in the mind of the Soviet for thirty years and we do not want to look at it . . . it is the extension of the Soviet Empire to the entire world."

—SALVADOR DE MADARIAGA

"We are not deceived, we deceive ourselves."

—WOLFGANG VON GOETHE

In January, 1961, between his election and his inauguration, John Fitzgerald Kennedy jokingly confided to an old friend: "If I had known as much about the world situation last summer as I do now, I would have voted for Nixon."

The thirty-fifth President of the United States had good grounds for such uneasiness. Things had not gone as his predecessors intended.

Since the end of World War Two, America had maintained garrisons and mighty fleets overseas, fought in the name of the United Nations a bitter little war in Korea, staged a show of strength in Lebanon, given military advice and assistance to a large number of friendly countries. It had made alliances with over forty other governments (shades of George Washington!).

It had disbursed no less than eighty-six billion dollars in foreign military and economic aid. And since the end of the Korean War the military budget had hovered around forty billion dollars a year.

On the other hand, far from trying to crush the Communist challenge and after only a brief attempt at roll-back, successive Administrations had steadily sought compromise and reconciliation. The United States had pursued peace and friendship as well as freedom and had been ready to pay for them. Aside from ethical considerations, the consequences of two world wars in one generation and the anxious forecast of a third had destroyed any enthusiasm for another "trial of arms." F.D.R.'s dream of a peaceful world policed by the cooperative efforts of major powers sharing the same strategic bases was America's first response to the new age's need.

Truman's refusal to coerce either the Soviets or the Chinese Communists with his monopoly of the atomic bomb reflected the deepest feelings of people everywhere. So did his Korean decision to curb (but not punish) aggression, in the name, not of the United States, but of the United Nations.

Eisenhower's retreat from Dulles' policy of liberation reflected not merely a warrior's repudiation of further bloodshed and a business-inspired yen for national economy, but a realization that science had in sober truth made nuclear war "unthinkable." What decent man would not "go anywhere in search of peace"? What normally sane human being would not agree that "some way must be found of living with the Russians"?

Who could deny that modern technology and communications, as well as a growing sense of human solidarity, *demanded* that modern nations control and somehow reduce their weapons, their ambitions and some of their precious sovereignty?

The American people had, furthermore, favored the liberation of all colonies and had welcomed new states into the United

Nations. By 1961 only the U.S.S.R. and Red China were left of the empires that had once encompassed the earth. The U.S. Administration had been lavish with help to the undeveloped countries. After all, how could any but the most hard-shelled "colonialist" refuse to welcome, even when he might seek to moderate, the rush of the undeveloped colonial peoples toward human dignity and equality of status? How deride their primitive, pathetic, anachronistic yet natural urge to become fully independent nations, free from outside interference?

In its recognition of all these aims, the United States had tried hard to eliminate "power politics." By signing the United Nations Charter and renouncing aggression and by accepting the Act of Rio which forbid intervention in the internal affairs of another American state, the United States had not only ruled out a preemptive strike against a Soviet Union morally capable of launching such a strike, but also any quick action to halt Soviet infection in the Western Hemipshere.

In a series of decisions (F.D.R.'s refusal to let General Hodges occupy Berlin, Truman's abstention from seeking victory in Korea, Eisenhower's promise "as a soldier" not to attack the U.S.S.R. unless first attacked, his further announcement that the United States would not intervene to help the embattled Hungarians, his renunciation of more U-2 flights over the U.S.S.R., to mention only a few) the United States had tied its own hands. As early as 1946 Truman offered to internationalize an atomic weapon of which he was then the sole possessor. Eisenhower stopped nuclear tests without any precautionary supervision at a time when tests were leading to a production of "cleaner" nuclear weapons that could eliminate much of the curse of nuclear war. He persevered in negotiations for arms control with an adversary obviously stalling for time in which to outproduce a drowsy America in guided missiles.

Yet somehow or other the effort had been of no avail. As

Khrushchev boasted to the Moscow Conference (1960), in spite of their efforts the imperialists lately "had not succeeded in involving a single new state in their military alignments." Meanwhile the Communist complex had grown from a single vast but impoverished country, Russia, to a great Red empire. Thirty-six million Communists, organized in about ninety "national" parties, ruled absolutely more than a billion non-Communists and had good prospects of acquiring additional millions of subjects.

American prestige, great in 1945 and rising to a peak with Truman's decision to defend Korea, was in slow decline. According to a poll of some "friendly" peoples (August, 1960), fifty per cent of Filipino students and forty-four per cent of all Britons believed that, given twenty or twenty-five years more of "peaceful coexistence," the U.S.S.R. would be stronger than the United States. The very improbability of such a development made the belief in it by tried and friendly allies the more startling.

Why was the free world losing? Not for any lack of means. All this time, America and its forty allies far surpassed their adversaries in potential material power.

Not for lack of information. News stories concerning Communism and the U.S.S.R., articles, broadcasts, committee reports, analyses, volumes profound or superficial, dull or delightful, perceptive or plain silly, poured out unendingly. Western governments dealt constantly with Soviet rulers, Western observers visited the Soviet empire in an unending flow. And the one thing that no foreigner could learn by personal contacts, analysis or observation of Communist societies—namely, *the precise future intention of Mr. K. and Mr. Mao*—this was set forth by Communist spokesmen as frankly as Adolf Hitler had revealed his purpose in *Mein Kampf*.

Khrushchev and Mao had not become leaders of their respective domains in order to preside over the liquidation of their common empire. Nor was there the slightest indication that they had abandoned or toned down their basic design of an all-Red world. Nor could anyone be sure that at a favorable moment they would not attempt to break the stalemate of terror by open attack.

U.S. leaders, while ruefully admitting all this, still chose to act on *totally different assumptions*, exactly as they had done ever since World War Two. In fact, the stronger the Communist bloc became, the less ready seemed successive Administrations to scrap a bankrupt strategy. In 1956, after two full years of discussion, a group of leading citizens headed by the former Assistant Secretary of War and High Commissioner to Germany, John J. McCloy, confessed its inability to choose between recommending a "forward or advancing" U.S. policy that aimed at recovering lost ground, and a policy of holding the line, *since neither was sure.*

Four years later, the monumental *Senate Compilation of Studies on U.S. Foreign Policy* made by thirteen research organizations (the current substitutes for statesmen) recommended little more than a continuation of the policy that was failing. Nor did the report of President Eisenhower's Commission on National Goals (December, 1960) reveal any awareness that the United States had slumped into a perilous morass from which it could extricate itself only by tremendous effort.

The causes of this predicament were several—among them, optimism based upon the nation's past success; the complacency of a "have" society that resented diverting money from personal consumption into a "wasteful" armament race; an incurable belief in the good will and similarity of men; Christian and humanitarian feeling; growing fear of war.

But the chief cause of the nation's failure to deal successfully with the Communist problem was *self-deception*. Kennedy's three predecessors had had access to all the facts—and had chosen to disbelieve or ignore them. Inescapably, therefore, to rally the West, turn retreat into advance and slow defeat into victory, the new President must first *put an end to make-believe. He must abandon the facile hopes of the previous twenty years, relinquish delusions* and brush aside the prevailing fog of wishful thinking.

Precisely, he had to recognize that the problem was not the world-wide revolution, or the discrepancy between rich and poor, or the surge of former colonies to independence. *It was Communism.* Next, before he could rally the non-Communist world to successful struggle, he had to persuade it of the true nature of the enemy.

Communism was not just a group of countries, one of them equipped with H-bombs and superior rockets. It was not a normal ideology or traditional "religion." Nor was it principally a new pattern of economic organization. It embraced these, but it was more. Essentially it was an international power conspiracy whose members were fanatically devoted to destroying the traditional pattern of civilization everywhere and replacing it by a totalitarian organization of society that turned men into ants.[1]

Communism's expansion was not another classic case of imperialism but a desperate undertaking by a magnificently organized international group animated by a purpose incompatible with that of traditional humanity. Between Soviet society and the open society no lasting compromise was possible, nor would Communists desist from their overriding purpose until compelled to do so. They had to be exhausted or defeated. Meanwhile, the free world's efforts to achieve genuine peaceful coexistence or a satisfying modus vivendi were vain. Communism regarded international agreements, in Eisenhower's words, as "scraps of paper"; the Soviet Union and Red China had broken hundreds of them. Among the alternatives open to free men, waging the Cold War

[1] Charles Malik, in an address at Williamsburg, Va., July 11, 1960: "The communist movement wants to overthrow every existing government regime, system, outlook, religion and philosophy and bring the whole world, all humane thought, aspiration, action and organization under its control. This is their declared, unchanged and unchanging objective."

was not the worst but the best available. The path to freedom was the only path to an acceptable peace.[2]

The world was involved in a power struggle of an entirely new type. The means were no longer military and economic alone. They included all forms of human activity and thought. The stake was not personal or national power. It was the power to determine the fate of the world.

Communism had understood this for over a hundred years. Its insistence on the inevitability of a *world order* had caught the imagination of millions. Twentieth Century technology, it argued, had, for the first time in history, made such an order both *possible* and *necessary* for the preservation of peace. Thanks to this precise promise, tyrannical Communism had attracted not only the power-hungry and those who wanted a fuller material life, but any number of idealists who would otherwise have been repelled by the cruelty of its methods. The prospect of a peaceful world order appealed particularly to small, weak and undeveloped lands. They hoped for rapid modernization and development and wanted to avoid the risks of any kind of war, hot or cold, while enjoying its benefits—assistance from both sides and ultimate military protection by America, if necessary.

This was another part of the Communist problem which the free peoples had persistently refused to face.

Yet, all in all, while the task of vanquishing Communism was formidable, it could still be done. The free nations had the means, provided they developed and used them. What they principally needed was greater unity, determination and political imagination.

Militarily, they were still far stronger than their adversaries. For all Eisenhower's economy, the United States was far from

[2] C. Burton Marshall, opening address to the American Political Science Association, Philadelphia, Sept. 8, 1960: "Those who proclaim the danger of continuing the Cold War have the matter precisely upside down. The danger lies in giving it up—abdicating the field to communist purpose."

being a "paper tiger" (though it sometimes acted like one). If necessary, it could *double* its military effort without serious inconvenience. It could do so, realizing that the current balance of terror was unstable and temporary and could be tipped in favor of freedom.

West Europe alone was superior to the U.S.S.R. in population, production, technology and potential military power. "Cleaner bombs," civilian shelters [3] (if serious arms control proved to be out of reach), pooled nuclear weapons, spy satellites opening the Communist lands to inspection and nullifying the chance of undetected preparation for a first strike—these would make nuclear war ever less likely, ever less destructive. The genuine pooling of Western science would enormously increase the chance of a decisive break-through in defensive weapons. If Western scientists spent half as much time working together as they spent in anxiously discussing the chances of peace with their (hand-picked) Soviet counterparts, they could hardly fail to get the jump upon the latter.

A reasonable Western expenditure on the most modern and standardized conventional weapons sufficient to repel non-nuclear attack in any part of the world would go far to reassure peoples rendered unsteady by a feeling of helplessness. In the Middle East and the Far East, allies like Turkey, Pakistan, Thailand, the Philippines and Japan could, if brought together and reinforced, put a stop to the marauding of Red China. The advantage was still on their side.

Any way one looked at it, the free world could survive, provided it achieved real unity of policy. Not necessarily identity of action or of propaganda, merely the decision never again to be *unintentionally* at odds, as at Suez or on the question of Formosa. Without doubt they could best negotiate as a bloc, enter into any

[3] See the argument in favor of shelters by Thomas K. Finletter in *Foreign Policy, the Next Phase.*

desirable agreements with Communists as a bloc, wage fully orchestrated political, economic and propaganda war as a bloc, give joint aid to undeveloped non-aligned peoples, and if necessary fight as a bloc. In short, they had to *appear* as well as to *be* indivisible. United they had nothing to fear.

For however menacing its stance and blustering its tone, regardless of the U.S.S.R.'s occasional scientific firsts and Red China's numbers, the Communist bloc was organically weak. It needed the momentum of constant success to survive. It was seeking to establish social conditions and a political regime repugnant to human nature and to human dignity. It lacked the support of many, perhaps of all, of its subject peoples. It required unending brainwashing and a vast expenditure of energy to keep its "conditioned" millions from revolt.

It was short of food. Soviet agriculture was hardly more productive than under the czars. In China, the people's communes had brought about the worst famine of the century. Never in their long history of submission to tyranny had the Chinese people endured such misery, and such governmental hypocrisy.

Red Russia was honeycombed with racial prejudice and anti-Semitism. A section of its youth was self-seeking and indifferent to doctrine. The national minorities were increasingly aware of themselves as Russian colonies. As the last remaining empire, the U.S.S.R. could one day fall victim to its own anti-colonial propaganda—provided the West helped.

Both the Iron Curtain and the Bamboo Curtain could be pierced by Western spokesmen employing all available means. Western governments, in their anxiety to reach an accommodation with the U.S.S.R., had silently suffered unending Communist charges of imperialism without loudly insisting that of all existing colonial "exploitation," that of the Soviet Union was the worst. The West had in fact barely whispered its demand that the Soviet minorities be allowed the same right of self-determination and secession that was being granted to other colonies.[4]

A West that set itself the task would have little difficulty in whipping up a dozen vociferous demands for independence in various parts of the U.S.S.R. (and to a lesser degree, in Red China). It could also help channel the latent hostility of the satellite countries into a vast movement of economic slowdown and sabotage. It could convince the Russian people of its aims—freedom as well as peace—and assure them of its friendship. It could bore successfully from within. Its first real victories were almost sure to bring out the latent doctrinal disputes, personal jealousies and national rivalries among comrades which their common success was keeping under control.

Compared with Communist weakness, that of the free world was overwhelmingly psychological. To put an end to make-believe and secure the adoption of a forward strategy an American President had to persuade his own and his allies' peoples that such a strategy was both necessary and safer than retreat. Defeatism in the West had made deep inroads. Nuclear pacifism, hardly distinguishable from appeasement, was growing. Western policy planners were divided into those who sought victory and those still devoted to compromise.

West Europe, for various reasons, was relying militarily far too much upon the United States. Instead of uniting, Britain and the continental Six were feuding over future markets. A few European leaders were already considering what to do when the United States "withdrew from Europe." Some citizens were slyly hoping for a chance to wriggle out of the costly and terrifying "duel between the two giants." Elsewhere the free world was threatened by the defection of once-faithful allies. The United States seemed

[4] At the Bandung conference of Asian-African countries in 1955, some states called attention to the Soviet's "neo-colonialism" in East Europe but not to its many *internal* colonies.

almost to prefer that the undeveloped states remain non-aligned. The assumption was that they could (or would) better defend their independence as neutrals than as allies of the world's most powerful country. Communism, on the other hand, had a place for every newcomer, and once in, he never got out.

In contrast, America seemed wedded to a status quo which hundreds of millions of people found unsatisfactory. On a planet bursting with new and startling possibilities, its traditional social structure shattered by technology, two world wars and widespread revolution, most American planners still thought in terms of rival sovereign states, which traditionally had never kept the peace for long.

This time it would be different, the planners insisted, and pointed to their unfailing support of the United Nations. Their policy satisfied some of the undeveloped peoples who cherished the United Nations as a forum that vastly exaggerated both their national voice and their strength, but it fooled few students of world politics. Adlai Stevenson might laud the United Nations as "the only hope of the world for peace and security." Actually it assured the world of neither. Its very universality, as well as its cautiously worded charter, drastically limited its capacity for law enforcement even if there had been any universally recognized law to enforce. As the meeting place of two irreconcilable power blocs, it was bound to remain another battlefield in the Cold War. No matter how many small nations wedded to non-alignment became members, they could not make the organization a "third force for peace," still less for freedom.

Clearly the Communist bloc had no intention of allowing any "mixed" world organization to acquire a power of its own that it might use to thwart the "inevitable" march toward an all-Red world. The veto-wielding Kremlin wanted no security for any but Communist members. Outside its own domains—in Latin-America, in the Middle East, in Southeast Asia—its goal was disorder.

Even while they admitted this, champions of the U.N. referred to the force of "world opinion." Since Moscow relied so heavily upon propaganda, it must value the United Nations as the world's most famous loudspeaker.

Unfortunately for this thesis, the United Nations of 1961 did not truly express world opinion. In the undeveloped countries, most people had no precise political opinions. The inhabitants of Communist-ruled countries dared not express the opinions they held. The one-state, one-vote rule in the General Assembly (where the U.S.S.R. had three) distorted the character of both debates and resolutions. Worst of all, while civilized states did usually manifest a "decent respect for the opinions of mankind," the Soviet Union habitually vetoed or ignored any U.N. resolutions that it disliked and refused to pay its share of the cost of U.N. activities it disapproved of. The other Communist states mechanically followed Moscow's lead, generally supported by some of the non-aligned nations.

The conclusion was obvious: *until all major governments* accepted the same kind of world, the United Nations was no effective alternative to the Communist world state.

To thwart the Communist's world plan, the free countries had to offer something of their own, similar but better. Nothing prevented them from unfurling a new banner to which all men could eventually repair, including those temporarily under the red flag, namely, *the promise of a world order as free as it was peaceful*, and taking a first step toward it. This could be an organization open to all like-intentioned peoples. The United States could start by combining its existing alliances into a free community, the growing nucleus of a coming free world order. This organization could check the current trend toward non-alignment. It could invite neutral peoples either to join and enjoy the common benefits, or stay out and enjoy fewer benefits with no certainty of protection.

Many Americans felt the need of a better defined national purpose. Creating a free and peaceful world order was a national and human purpose daring enough to satisfy the most idealistic as well as the most realistic of spirits.[5]

"Integration" was in the air. In the Thirties, Clarence Streit launched the idea of a "federation of democracies," a "union of the free." Most students of government now realized that no single country, however powerful and rich, could solve its problems alone.

Six West European nations were moving from a customs union toward greater political unity. The United States had encouraged this European "integration," but had remained out of it. Nonetheless Americans, too, had gone a long way since 1945. In 1960, John K. Jessup upset nobody by conjecturing in *Life* magazine that "national states might no longer be the most meaningful integers of creative political thought."

Many in the West advocated the consolidation of NATO, with policy-making organs of its own. Nelson A. Rockefeller urged the United States to go about creating three confederations, North Atlantic, Western Hemisphere and African. Most significant, Congress in the summer of 1960 passed an act authorizing the calling of a convention of "representative citizens" to explore the possibilities of greater political and economic unity and report back by January 31, 1962. From these projects to the conscious creation of a Free Community as the nucleus of a free world order (perhaps ultimately merged with a transformed United Nations) was no great distance.

Given a forward strategy, a Free Community would meet the

[5] See *Prospect for America*—The Rockefeller Panel Reports, 1960, ". . . the task that history has imposed upon us . . . is . . . helping to shape a new world order in all its dimensions, spiritual, economic, political, social." Also, Townsend Hoopes, "The Persistence of Illusion," *Yale Review*, March, 1960, "We are engaged in a contest to see who shall construct the new world order. . . . Our aim cannot be less than a *novus ordo seclorum* (the motto . . . on the Great Seal of the United States)."

Communist challenge squarely and as a unit. How far its members would need to unite and what common institutions they would develop were problems that could best be solved in the light of actual experience.

Traditionalists in the West opposed all such "supernational" ideas. They considered "polarization" by the free world unnecessary, provocative, Utopian. (India might not like it, they argued. African "nationalists" would howl.) But they could not alter the probability that united in a Free Community, the non-Communist states could best thwart Khrushchev's promise to "make them dance like fish in a frying pan." They could not deny that while they appeased and waited, Communism was slowly eating its way across the planet like a sinister cancer and that the free nations of the West, despite their superior resources, had found no way to stop it.

Clearly it was time for a change in their strategy. As a nucleus of a coming world order, the free states could properly undertake collective intervention, whether to assist peoples revolting against Communist tyranny or to eliminate Castro-ism from the Western Hemisphere.

President Kennedy might still hesitate before deciding to raise his sights so high. He might, as he did in his inaugural address, again appeal to "those who would make themselves our adversary" to renew the quest for peace "before the dark powers of destruction unleashed by science engulf all humanity in planned or accidental self-destruction." Nevertheless, he could not but bump his nose against the hard fact that to the Kremlin peaceful coexistence meant simply "acquiescence by others to Soviet designs." [6]

The world stood at the threshold of a new era. To many long-

[6] C. Burton Marshall, *idem.* Zhukov said in London on February 24, 1961, "We have declared and will declare again . . . that the peaceful coexistence of ideas is as nonsensical as fried snowballs."

submerged peoples it seemed the light of a new dawn. Communists were making the most of the opportunity. Were America and its allies to stand by while their enemy made the new age his own? The West did not need better cards. It needed bolder, better players. In two world wars the democracies had reached their best at moments of greatest danger. They had produced leaders who demanded the most of them. In his inaugural address John Fitzgerald Kennedy had recognized this.

"In the long history of the world," he said, "only a few generations have been granted the role of defending freedom in its hour of maximum danger. I do not shrink from this responsibility—I welcome it. I do not believe that any of us would exchange places with any other people or any other generation. The energy, the faith, the devotion, which we bring to this endeavor will light our country and all who serve it—and the glow from that fire can truly light the world."

So spoke President Kennedy. The need was for greatness. The field was wide open.

FOR FURTHER READING

For readers who wish to pursue this subject, either to confirm or contest the author's conclusions, I submit a partial list of sources. Starred items were particularly helpful to me.

General

The Autobiography of Lincoln Steffens, Harcourt Brace, 1931; Bemis, Samuel Flagg: *A Diplomatic History of the United States,* Holt, New York, 1936; Stimson: *On Active Service in Peace and War,* Harper and Brothers, 1948; Kennan, George F.: *American Diplomacy 1900-1950,* University of Chicago Press, Chicago, 1951*; Elliott, William Yandell: *Foreign Policy, Its Organization and Control,* Columbia University Press, 1952; Pratt, Julius W.: *A History of United States Foreign Policy,* Prentice-Hall, 1955; Williams, William Appleman: *The Shaping of American Diplomacy,* Rand MacNally, 1956; Crowley, W. D.: *The Background to Current Affairs,* Macmillan, London, 1958; Davids, Jules: *America and the World of Our Times,* Random House, 1960*; *United States Foreign Policy,* prepared under the direction of the Committee on Foreign Relations, U.S. Senate, 1960; Walsh, Edmund A.: *Total Power,* Doubleday, 1948; Spanier, John W.: *American Foreign Policy Since World War Two,* Praeger, 1960*.

Chapters I, II, and III

Dennis, A. L. P.: *The Foreign Policies of Soviet Russia,* Dutton, 1924; Knickerbocker, H. R.: *The Red Trade Menace,* Dodd, Mead, 1931; Steffens, Lincoln: *The Autobiography of,* Harcourt Brace, 1931; Schuman, Frederick L.: *American Policy Toward Russia Since 1917,* International Publishers, 1928; Hull, Cordell: *The Memoirs of,* Macmillan, 1948*; Farley, James A.: *The Roosevelt Years,* Whittlesey House, 1948*; *The Foreign Relations of the United States:* Soviet

Union, 1933-1939, Government Printing Office, 1952; Chambers, Whittaker: *Witness,* Random House, 1952.

Chapter IV

Davies, Joseph E.: *Mission to Moscow,* Simon and Schuster, 1941; Lippmann, Walter: *U.S. Foreign Policy; Shield of the Republic,* Little Brown, 1943; Welles, Sumner: *The Time for Decision,* Harper and Brothers, 1944*; Roosevelt, Elliott: *As He Saw It,* Duell, Sloan and Pearce, 1948* (the most revealing of all sources on F.D.R.'s views); Sherwood, Robert E.: *Roosevelt and Hopkins,* Harper and Brothers, 1948*; Eisenhower, Dwight D.: *Crusade in Europe,* Doubleday, 1948; Leahy, William D.: *I Was There,* Whittlesey House, 1950; Churchill, Winston: *The Second World War:* Vol. III, *The Grand Alliance,* Vol. IV, *The Hinge of Fate,* 1950, Vol. V, *Closing the Ring,* 1951*; Bradley, Omar N.: *A Soldier's Story,* Henry Holt, 1951.

Chapter V

Byrnes, James F.: *Speaking Frankly,* Harper and Brothers, 1947; Helm, William P.: *Harry Truman,* Duell, Sloan and Pearce, 1947; McNaughton and Heymeyer: *Harry Truman, President,* Whittlesey House, 1948; Millis, Walter, edited by: *The Forrestal Diaries,* The Viking Press, 1951* (admirable); Churchill, Winston: *The Second World War,* Vol. VI, *Triumph and Tragedy,* Houghton Mifflin, 1953*.

Chapters V, VI

Truman, Harry S.: *Year of Decision,* Vol. I, 1955, and *Years of Trial and Hope,* Vol. II, 1956, Doubleday*.

Chapter VI

Linebarger, Paul M. A.: *The China of Chiang Kai-shek,* World Peace Foundation, 1941*; White, Theodore H. and Jacoby, Annalee: *Thunder Out of China,* William Sloane Associates, 1946; Valco, Francis: *The China White Paper,* Library of Congress Legislation Reference Service, 1949; *Relations With China,* Department of State,

1949; Tong, Hollington, K.: *Chiang Kai-shek,* China Publishing Company, Taipei, 1953; Feis, Herbert: *The China Tangle,* Princeton University Press, 1953; Senate Foreign Relations Committee Documents, 1943-1953: *The U.S. and the Korean Problem,* Government Printing Office, 1953; *Inquiry Into the Military Situation of the Far East and Facts Surrounding the Relief of General of The Army Douglas MacArthur from His Assignment in the Area,* Senate Armed Service and Foreign Relations Committee, 5 vols., Government Printing Office, 1951*; Romanus, Charles F. and Riley, Sunderland: *United States Army in World War II: China-Burma–India Theater, Stilwell's Command Problems,* Office of the Chief of Military History, Department of the Army, Government Printing Office, 1956*; Chiang Kai-shek: *Soviet Russia in China,* Farrar, Straus, 1958; Wedemeyer, Albert C.: *Wedemeyer Reports,* Holt, 1958*; U.S. Department of State, Historical Division: *American Foreign Policy 1950-1955,* Government Printing Office, 1957.

Chapters VII and VIII

Dulles, John Foster: *War or Peace,* Macmillan, 1950*; Gunther, John: *Eisenhower: The Man and the Symbol,* Harper, 1951; Smith, Merriman: *Meet Mr. Eisenhower,* Harper, 1954; Donovan, Robert J.: *Eisenhower: The Inside Story,* Harper, 1956; Pusey, Merlo J.: *Eisenhower the President,* Macmillan, 1956; Childs, Marquis: *Eisenhower: Captive Hero,* Harcourt, Brace, 1958; The Rockefeller Brothers Special Studies Project: *The Mid-Century Challenge to U.S. Foreign Policy,* Doubleday, 1959; U.S. Department of State, Historical Division: *Current Documents,* 1956, and *President Eisenhower's European Trip,* both Government Printing Office, 1959; Drummond, Roscoe and Coblentz, Gaston: *Duel at the Brink,* Doubleday, 1960*; Stebbins, Richard P.: *The United States in World Affairs,* 1959, and Zinner, Paul E.; edited by: *Documents on American Foreign Relations,* 1959, both by Harper, 1960; Tournoux, J. R.: *Secrets d' Etat,* Plon, Paris, 1960; Smith, Merriman: *A President's Odyssey,* Harper, 1961.

Chapter IX

Hughes, John Emmet: *America the Vincible,* Doubleday, 1959; Sulzberger, C. L.: *What's Wrong With U.S. Foreign Policy,* Harcourt Brace, 1959; Seton-Watson, Hugh: *Neither War Nor Peace,* Praeger,

1960*; Bennet, John C.: *Christianity and Communism Today*, Association Press, 1960; Plamenatz, John; *On Alien Rule and Self-Government*, Longmans, Green, London, 1960; Lukacs, John: *A History of the Cold War*, Doubleday, 1961*.

Chapter X

Rostow, W. W.: *The Dynamics of Soviet Society*, Vol. I., M.I.T., 1952; Sulzberger, C. L.: *The Big Thaw*, Harper, 1956; Tran-Tam: *Communism and War in Asia*, Free Pacific Editions, Saigon, 1959*; Schuman, Frederick L.: *Russia Since 1917*, Knopf, 1957; Rauch, Georg von: *A History of Soviet Russia*, Praeger, 1954; Department of State: *Soviet World Outlook—A Handbook of Communist Statements*, Government Printing Office, 1959*; Goodman, Elliott R.: *The Soviet Design for a World State*, Columbia University Press, 1960*; Novak, Joseph: *The Future is Ours, Comrade*, Doubleday, 1960*; Chow Ching-wen: *Ten Years of Storm*, Holt, Rinehart and Winston, 1960; Deutscher, Isaac: *The Great Contest; Russia and the West*, Oxford University Press, 1960; Mosely, Philip: *The Kremlin and World Politics*, Vintage Books, 1960*; Dallin, David J.: *Soviet Foreign Policy After Stalin*, Lippincott, 1961*; *The Cold War Manifesto—an Analysis of the Declaration Issued on 6 December, 1960 After the Three-Week Moscow Meeting of 81 Communist Parties*, NATO Letter, February, 1961*; Gibney, Frank: *The Khrushchev Pattern*, Duell, Sloan and Pearce, 1960; Overstreet, Harry and Bonaro: *The War Called Peace*, Norton, 1961; *December 6, 1960 Statement of the Moscow Conference of Representatives of Communist and Workers Parties and the Krushchev Report on the Moscow Conference of Representatives of Communist and Workers Parties*, Foreign Broadcast Information Service, Daily Report Supplements*; Meyer, Frank S.: *The Moulding of Communists*, Harcourt Brace, 1960.

Chapter XI

Kahn, Herman: *On Thermonuclear War*, Princeton University Press, 1960*; Fowler, John M., edited by: *Fallout*, Basic Books, 1960; "Special Report on Arms Control," *Business Week*, March 18, 1961; *Potential for Expansion of National Security Programs*, Stanford Research Institute, October, 1960; Special Issue, Arms Control,

Daedalus, Wesleyan University Press, 1960; Baar and Howard: *Polaris!,* Harcourt, Brace, 1960; Bergaust, Erik: *Reaching for the Stars,* Doubleday, 1960.

Chapter XII

Finletter, Thomas K.: *Foreign Policy: The Next Phase, The 1960's,* Harper 1958, 1960; Campaigne, Jameson G.: *American Might and Soviet Myth,* Regnery, 1960; Madariaga, Salvador de: *The Blowing Up of the Parthenon or How to Lose the Cold War,* Praeger, 1960; Strausz-Hupé, Kintner and Possony: *A Forward Strategy for America,* Harper, 1961*.

Index